Albert H. Heusser was a resident of Passaic and visited many former Indian sites throughout New York and New Jersey. In *Homes and Haunts of the Indians* he takes you on a personal tour to the many places where he discovered Native-American artifacts. Here are some of the locations featured in the book:

New York
Cuddebackville
Greenwood Lake
Manhattan
Mt. Vernon
Niagara Falls
Palisades
Shawangunk Mountains
Staten Island
Stony Point
Tuxedo
White Plains

New Jersey
Cedar Pond
Echo Lake
Fort Lee
Greenwood Lake
Hackensack
Ho-Ho-Kus
Hunterdon
Macopin Lake
Montclair
Pascack
Passaic
Paterson
Ramapo Mountains
Trenton

INDIAN ROCK-SHELTER
NEAR GREENWOOD LAKE, PASSAIC CO., N. J.

(Photo. by Mr. F. J. Welles)

HOMES AND HAUNTS
OF THE
INDIANS:
NEW YORK AND NEW JERSEY

BY
ALBERT H. HEUSSER

HVA Press
Warwick, NY

Published by HVA Press

This edition copyright © 2019 by HVA Press, LLC

Homes and Haunts of the Indians was first published in 1923.

This book was scanned from an early edition of the original work. The interior scan of this book is the property of HVA Press, LLC. All rights reserved.

The HVA logo is a trademark of HVA Press, LLC.

Cover design by Daniel Rembert

Print ISBN: 978-1-948697-04-0

Manufactured in the United States of America

HVA Press
Warwick, NY
HVAPress.com

FOREWORD

The story of aboriginal man, treated from the scientific standpoint of Prof. Henry Fairfield Osborn, is an anthropological education in itself, adequately supplemented by our public exhibits of prehistoric life and art, first and foremost among which is that of the American Museum of Natural History in New York City. Longfellow has perpetuated the American Indian in poetry; Dr. Charles Conrad Abbott has treated the subject in much the same delectable fashion as did John Burroughs his wild creatures of fur and feathers; and Prof. John D. Prince has, with others, delved into the intricacies of the language of the red-skins. The pages which follow are neither profoundly scientific nor rhetorically elegant. They are the recorded observations and delights of one who has endeavored to lift the veil of the prosaic present and visualize the picturesque prehistoric days and doings in his own restricted locality—the regions in New York and New Jersey contiguous to Manhattan Island. Scarcely a community throughout the length and breadth of our country is devoid of similar traces of the so-called "Indians" or the little-known people who preceded them, and the mission of this little pamphlet (and I am told that every book should have a mission) is to bring into the lives of those who may read it a new joy—the joy of neighborhood archaeology. Being fully aware of the fact that local conditions vary greatly, I am nevertheless persuaded that no one, be he a resident of Portland, Maine, or San Diego, California, need fear a sterile field of endeavor. Well-nigh every portion of our great country still holds a store of hidden treasure which may be found by those who search aright. Mayhap some suggestions of mine will cause a seeking and a finding of traces of the by-gone people. One admonition only may I presume to offer. If success crowns the effort of any amateur anthropologist whom I may inspire, let him remember that his collection of specimens should be intelligently labeled and arranged in an orderly fashion. Moreover, when he shall have done with them forever, their place should be a public museum—not the trunk, the attic or the discard. It should be a thought uppermost in the mind of every collector, whether of books, manuscripts, or curios, that his treasures would make a most appropriate gift to the public. With this in mind, his pleasure should be two-fold: the joy of possession for himself, and the anticipated reward of bequeathing the fruits of his labors as a legacy of information and pleasure to future generations.

Albert H. Heusser

Paterson, N. J.,
    Sept. 22nd, 1923.

TABLE OF CONTENTS

PAGES

CHAPTER I 1- 18

Initial excursions in search of Indian relics.—Aboriginal trails.—Water-courses and camp sites.—Indian farms and village sites.—The primitive worker of flint and his product.—Antiquity of Indian artifacts.—Friendly intercourse between settler and Indian.—David Godwin's diary.—The science of archaeology.—"Locust Lodge."

CHAPTER II 19- 40

Beside the brooks and rivulets.—The Indians as fishermen.—Canoes and "dugouts."—Fording places.—Cataracts.—Niagara.—The Falls of the Passaic.—Indian Reservations of to-day.—Shell deposits.—Indian feasting grounds.—Inwood.—The confraternity of those who comprehend.

CHAPTER III 41- 56

Appearance and characteristics of the Indians.—Peter Hasenclever's contemporary descriptions.—Indian communal life.—Village-site implements: the hoe, mortars and pestles, hand-hammers, axes, tomahawks and celts, "scrapers."—Migratory habits of the Indians.—Indian women.—Pottery.

CHAPTER IV 57- 70

The wilderness, natural environment of the redskin.—The mountain-top vantage points.—Seasons suitable for research.—The joys of the rambler.—Types of secondary rock-shelters and "occasional" habitations of the Indians.—"Bear Rock."—Darlington Rock-house.—The Lake Macopin shelter.—Garret Mountain "lean-to."

CHAPTER V 71- 88

Mr. Max Schrabisch and the exploration of aboriginal rock-shelters.—The Cedar Pond Rock.—Transient abodes of the Indians.—Farmers' dogs.—Ancient trails.—Civilization's changes.—The pleasures of companionship.—Indian council fires.—Smoke-stained rocks.—Golf Hill and "Man-of-War Rock."—The beauties of the Ramapo Mountains.—Revolutionary significance of the Ramapo defile.—"Horse-stable Rock."—Claudius Smith, the "Cowboy of the Ramapo Mountains."—The beauties of winter among the hills.

CHAPTER VI 91-105

Religious beliefs of the aboriginal Americans.—Ceremonial articles.—Knowledge of medicine and surgery possessed by primitive people.—Banner-stones and "gorgets."—Beads, wampum and pipes.—Trade articles.—The white-man's wampum.—Indian burials.—The vanished people and their well-beloved forest haunts.

It is with pleasure that the author acknowledges the inspiration and encouragement he has received from the monographs and discourses of

Mr. Max Schrabisch

ILLUSTRATIONS

(From photographs and pen-sketches by the author)

Indian Rock-shelter near Greenwood Lake, N. J.	Frontispiece
"Locust Lodge"	1
The Saddle River, Bergen Co., N. J.	5
The Pond, Ringwood Manor, N. J.	6
Flint Blade, Broken Arrow-heads and "Chips"	9
Arrow and Spear-heads	15
The Palisades of the Hudson	19
Indian Fording Place, Passaic River	23
Looking Across the Hudson River from Fort Lee	24
Niagara Falls	27
"Hiawatha, the Legendary Genius of the Onondagas"	28
Indian Dug-out Canoe	30
The Falls of the Passaic, Paterson, N. J.	33
The Bronx River, near White Plains, N. Y.	34
Ancient Tulip Tree at Inwood	37
The Falls of the Youghiogheny	38
Corn-bowl, Pestle, Celt and "Hand-hammer"	41
Old Cottage at Sneden's Landing, (N. Y.)	44
Indian Corn-bowls, Ringwood Manor, N. J.	45
"Tory Rock," which yielded no relics	48
Aged Elm at Hohokus, Bergen Co., N. J.	49
Stone Hatchet and Pottery Fragment	57
Bear Rock, Morris County, N. J.	59
Darlington Rock House	60
Polished Point and Bone Awl	62
The Rock-girt Covert at Lake Macopin	65
Garret Mountain Rock-shelter	66
Fragment of Iroquoian Pottery	68
"Cedar Pond Rock"	71
Detail of Cedar Pond Rock	75
"Golf Hill" Rock House	76
"Man-of-War Rock" (Tuxedo Park, N. Y.)	81
Beneath the Shelter of "Horse-stable Rock"	82
The Indian Kept in Remembrance	89
Site of Old "James Towne," Virginia	90
Banner-stones and "Gorget"	91
The Ringwood River	92
At Mount Vernon on the Potomac	96
Indian Ceremonial Pipe	97
Old Campbell Wampum Factory, (Pascack, N. J.)	99
Types of Indian Wampum	100

"Wrapt in the mist of ages, the story of the American aborigine is well nigh inscrutable. There being no written records to elucidate what apparently must always be beyond human ken, we should be hopelessly in the dark were it not for the researches of archaeology, that noble handmaid of history, which has so often proved valuable in shedding a stray ray of light into the dim past. Difficult as the archaeological method is and depending largely, as it does, upon the correct interpretation of meagre and minute clues, thus giving considerable scope to scientific imagination, the very elements of uncertainty attending it constitute in the eyes of its devotees its chief charm and fascination."

MAX SCHRABISCH.

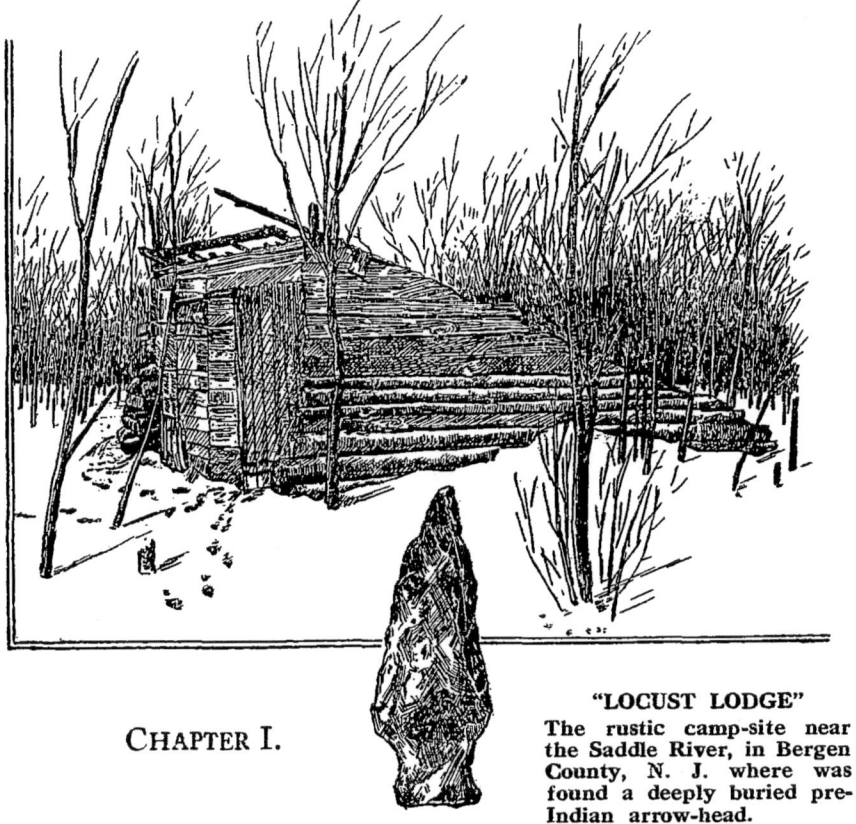

"LOCUST LODGE"
The rustic camp-site near the Saddle River, in Bergen County, N. J. where was found a deeply buried pre-Indian arrow-head.

CHAPTER I.

HOWEVER imperfect, the first "find" in the way of Indian handicraft ought never to be discarded. It may be but a crude fragment of worked flint, found beside a woodland trail, telling the simple story of a savage huntsman who, pausing in the chase, tarried for a moment to reshape his last remaining point. But in after life this memento of a maiden expedition to the haunts of the red men will mean much more: it will be a treasured keep-sake—in value far greater than later finds of rarity and beauty; the key, as it were, which opened the door to a new world of keen enjoyment and broadened vision.

In the by-gone days, when we were ignorant concerning these things—which are today equally mysterious to the uninitiated—we passed over many a choice specimen as we roamed across the newly-plowed fields of our rural neighbors. Perhaps we enjoyed our woodland rambles none the less because of this blissful lack of knowledge; certainly our childhood excursions were in no way marred because we knew not that the hillsides over which we scampered, or the alluring creek down in the valley, had been much frequented by the long-forgotten Indians. Yet, with new knowledge comes new possibility. Once you have come into possession of the few simple fundamentals of prehistoric research, you are enriched by a new source of profound pleasure. Recreational walks take on an instant and added charm, and you will find yourself enjoying in the familiar regions which you know and love, the same queer thrill of expectancy and satisfaction which comes to those who brave the perils of sea and desert and thick jungle to bring to light the treasures of the past from old world ruins. The location of a hitherto unknown Indian camp site beside the pond where, as a boy, you fished and swam in gay abandon, will be just as truly a scientific achievement as was the opening of the tombs of the Kings in the Valley of the Nile.

To me, Providence has been most kind. It has been my privilege to experience the traditional joys of travel in foreign lands, and in my comparisons I speak advisedly. I have gone down into the depths of some of the royal sepulchres of Egypt's pharaohs in the brown hills which fringe the desert to the west of the ancient Theban necropolis; I have gazed upon the withered face of Amenophis in his narrow and silent chamber with its star-studded ceiling; I have alighted from my camel to pick fragments of pottery and beads from the shifting sands which cover the ancient cemetery of Memphis; I have trodden the banks of the Jordan and the marble pavement of the Roman Forum; but the satisfaction was no whit greater than that which has accompanied dozens of expeditions to the much-frequented rendezvous of the aboriginal Americans, where, amid scenery the like of which for loveliness and beauty old Egypt never knew, I have found flint and pottery in sufficient abundance to satisfy my craving for archaeological specimens, besides communing with Nature in her loveliest aspects.

Moreover, these home-land rambles permit the companionship of friends like-minded and congenial; their cost is trifling; and they can be interspersed with refreshing frequency between those daily duties which are the portion of most men and women in this workaday world of endeavor and accomplishment.

The preparation of a primer upon the subject of "domestic anthropology," or the search for traces left by the American Indian, would be by no means difficult—at least that portion having to do with the determination of sites once favored by the red-men. Certain fundamental prerequisites usually determined the course of their woodland trails and the location of their much-frequented places of habitual resort.

Almost invariably, their favored highways followed the watercourses, for reasons readily apparent. Beside the streamlets and rivers which meandered tranquilly through vast expanses of virgin forest, the matter of beating an even pathway was a task of comparative ease, far more to the liking of the savage wanderer than an arduous and continual climbing over bowlder-strewn hills or through jungles of opposing thicket. The waterways themselves, when of sufficient extent, were the natural avenues of communication and travel, not only affording easy passage for sturdy dug-outs or canoes of delicate birch, but providing abundant means of sustenance. Fish, water-fowl and crustacea were so easily to be obtained that no tawny brave or hard-working squaw need fear the pangs of hunger while following a stream. Hence it is by the river-banks that the searcher will often find chips and artifacts reminiscent of the race which has passed from among us.

Fortunate, it is, indeed, that rivers decline to be disposed of and obliterated by man, the greatest enemy of Nature. Were it not so, there would no longer be anything unappropriated. As it is, I like to imagine the changeless rivers as still belonging to the simple-minded folk who named them, long ago, in unwritten and musical syllables. The Kennebec, the Passaic, the Cuyahoga—thousands of such streams beloved by the children of the forest—preserve for us a heritage which may not be taken away.

Slight elevations of the terrain at the meeting places of brooklet and river are seldom found to be devoid of flint flakes, shells, and charred bones, attesting to the oft-repeated tarryings of aboriginal hunters and fishermen. In fact, so far as "surface finds" are concerned, I know of no more fruitful fields for exploration than the "high-spots" by the rivers. Almost invariably the oft-plowed fields of river-side farmers seem once to have been utilized for similar purposes by the primitive people who preceded their settler-ancestors. Possibly the Indians originally made these very clearings and planted crops upon the same ground. In the case of supposed "village sites," arable land near at hand was a prime factor. Dependent in large measure, as were the red-skins, upon the spoils of the chase, they had learned by years of experience that the soil itself was an added source of abundant yield, and their farming operations were conducted with great sagacity,

THE SADDLE RIVER (Bergen County, N. J.)

Chill winter is not without its charms for the lover of the great out-doors. We dread its approach; and as the first snow falls, sigh for the summer that has passed. Yet Nature is exceeding wise, and, for those of us who cannot "Recuperate" in the vast silences of the Canadian Northwest, she sends year after year, the same crisp and invigorating tonic.

Covered by a blanket of white, our Indian fields assume a new aspect. Half-frozen, the streamlets beloved of the red-man still flow onward to the sea, and your winter photographs will be worth while, if for no other purpose than for comfort when next August comes around.

Along the Saddle River, as is the case with well-nigh every similar creek, ran a favored aboriginal trail, and quite often the bracing winter excursion, undertaken when obscuring foliage is no longer an obstacle, will reveal certain peculiarities of river-side landscape which will prove worth-while clues as to probable "sites" which, when studiously examined later on, will reward you handsomely.

THE POND, RINGWOOD MANOR
(Passaic Co., N. J.)

This illustration is given as showing a moderate elevation of the terrain, contiguous to water, such as would appeal to the Indians as being an ideal camp site. In numberless instances, lake or river-side situations of like character have proven to be prolific in aboriginal traces. Many Indian villages were similarly located.

A covering of turf, or well-kept greensward such as is seen in the foreground, precludes, of course, any attempt at diggng. But when such sites are utilized as farmland and are subjected to repeated ploughings, the toll of relics is really astonishing.

Incidentally this peaceful bit of landscape was enlivened, in 1781, by the transient bivouac of a contingent of French soldiers, en route to Yorktown from the Hudson Highlands. Some of them, who died in the service of King Louis, are buried beneath the grove at the right (middle distance), and here, also, sleeps worthy Robert Erskine, iron-master, friend of Washington, and Surveyor-General of the Continental armies.

measured, of course, by the standard of a maximum of increase with a minimum of physical labor. And the fields still retain a harvest ready for the industrious archaeologist. Well-nigh every intelligent farmer has a few arrow-heads, or perhaps a tomahawk, ensconced upon the shelves of the ornate "what-not" in his parlor —found "years ago," as he will tell you, upon his farm. But many little fragments have escaped the eye of the aforesaid hard-working farmer, for rarely is he constantly on the lookout for these things. Fertilizing and weeding, seed-sowing and harvest—these are his allotted portion, and he becomes indifferent after a while to all else save work and the dinner-bell. With due regard, then, for the tiller of the fields, may I suggest that his furrowed acres—in the months when no damage will be done to growing crops—offer wonderful possibilities. When the snows of winter have yielded to the genial sun of early spring, or after the heavy equinoctial rains have settled the dust and debris of summer, enter boldly into the domain of the husbandman and keep your eyes upon mother earth. If something interesting does not reward you, it will be a case of exceptional ill-luck. Chips you may confidently expect; if the field was once a village site where many implements were made, century after century, fragments of arrow-points, pitted hand-hammers, and grinding pestles will not be exceptional; while an occasional perfect specimen of arrow or spear-head (lost, we may conjecture, by some huntsman) will crown your day with keen delight.

So-called "chips" or "flakes"—which are the telltale clues identifying a locality as having been visited by the aborigines—are small fragments or slivers of stone broken off in the making of an implement. And the first lesson in this branch of wood-craft is supplied by the humble and well-nigh ubiquitous chip, which to know and recognize is the "open sesame" to the vast storehouse of treasure and pleasure incident to "Indian hunts" of today. In contradistinction to rounded pebbles and field stones, chips are invariably thin and slightly curved, and have edges of knife-like sharpness. To the primitive worker of flint they were the equivalent to the shavings of the whittler. Flint, jasper, argillite, and chert were found by the red-skins of the Eastern States to be the most desirable raw materials from which to fashion their weapon-heads; and the beautiful conchoidal fracture of the cast-off fragments attests to the workable qualities of the nodules upon which they chose to busy themselves. Quartz was not nearly so tractable, although in many localities where other minerals where conspicuous by their absence its use was quite common. Baser materials were availed of in a pinch—even bits of basaltic trap-rock and fine-textured sandstone—but the resulting artifacts as well as the cast-off fragments show that they were merely makeshifts. Incomparably superior to the best of flint was the obsidian of the West, in its beautiful jet-blackness or glossy red and brown. But few and far between are the specimens made from this *material par excellence* which have been found along the Atlantic coast; and these are at once recognized as foreign to the Coastal Algonquin; they were bartered, perhaps, and undoubtedly regarded as highly-prized possessions by their owners.

Acquaint yourself, then, first of all with the chip, as did the writer, when his eyes were opened a dozen years ago. Up to 1912, I had never seen an arrowhead, nor did I dream that so much of interest was to be found, literally, beside my own doorstep. My initiation into the mysteries of Indian lore came about as a logical consequence of attempting to prepare a lecture upon "Historic New Jersey." Naturally, the thought occurred that it would be well to preface my discourse with a few words concerning the aboriginal inhabitants of the Eastern American seaboard. At that time I knew but little of the American Indian, save to associate his name with traditional border warfare, and

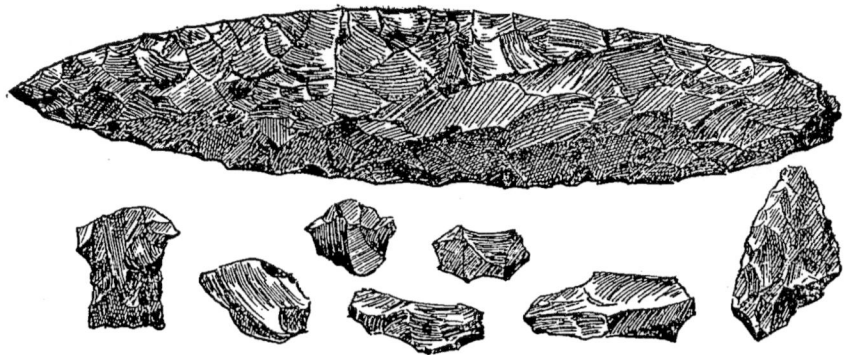

FINISHED FLINT BLADE, BROKEN ARROW-HEADS, and "CHIPS"

The five fragments shown in the lower center are typical of the so-called "chips" usually found in profusion on Indian camp sites. They are the cast-off slivers of flint or other workable material resulting from the manufacture of implements. The beautifully wrought knife illustrates a serviceable weapon, fashioned with infinite care. This specimen was found in Bergen County, N. J., and measures nearly six inches in length. The broken pieces at the left and right respectively, show the haft and the tip of two flint arrow-points found near the Passaic River at Paterson, N. J.

his likeness with such painted braves as I had seen in the delectable company of "Buffalo Bill" when his Wild West Circus came to town. Honestly acknowledging ignorance, I besought the aid of Mr. Max Schrabisch, whose researches and studies along this line were already beginning to bring him public recognition. With that willingness to assist which has ever characterized men of culture and attainment, he "took me in tow" and patiently taught me the alphabet of archaeology, opening my eyes like those of blind Bartimaeus— if not *with* the clay, certainly *from* the clay and the secrets it contained. It is but natural, then, that I pass on the key, and if my unpretentious observations serve to do a similar good turn for others, his efforts and mine will have been amply justified.

The making of an arrow-head, although requiring great skill, cannot be classed among the "lost arts," as there are many Indians living today who are capital artisans in this work; some of them were at the Jamestown Exposition, I am told. A few white men have acquired the knack, also; and in the Middle West there is an ingenious chap who makes his livelihood by counterfeiting the workmanship of the red-skin. Many specimens of his handiwork have been palmed off upon gullible collectors as genuine examples of prehistoric industry. Happily, the explorer who accumulates his collection bit by bit from his own findings here, there and at random, is safe from this sort of chicanery.

A flint flake, after having been cracked from a larger nodule, may be shaped and sharpened in several ways. It is possible to heat the bit of stone and then by carefully dropping water upon it, cause tiny flakes to fly off, until by continuing the operation the resulting implement bears some semblance to a point. The Indians, however, seem to have succeeded in flaking off tiny pieces exactly when and where they chose by applying pressure in a gentle and sliding manner by means of another stone or a piece of bone. Skillfully directed staccato blows might have answered the purpose in "roughing out" an artifact; but the savages found, by centuries of experience, that the best results were obtained by patience and gentleness—a lesson, by the way, which we, too, might apply in our dealings with ourselves and our fellow-men. Just as the inscrutable and silent Indian learned to make points and blades which are the marvel of archaeologists because of the fineness of their edges, so may we, by the application of an equal measure of the same spirit of painstaking care, produce results which will be worth the effort.

We are safe in holding to the belief that every Indian could fashion a stone tip for his feather-tailed arrow shaft of dogwood. Equally certain it is that some possessed a far greater measure of skill than others. Personally, I incline to the theory that there were "specialists" among them who made a business of the fashioning of flints, and who bartered their product for the necessaries of life, supplied by those of their dark-faced brothers who were less proficient in weapon-making than they.

I suppose every enthusiast upon this subject has speculated as to the age of the specimens which have come under his observation. I speak advisedly of the Indians who inhabited the regions contiguous to New York City when I say that the last of them departed about the time of the so-called French and Indian War. As to Paterson, N. J., my "home town," we have documentary evidence that they lingered in the vicinity up to a few years prior to the Revolution, and lived in peace and friendliness as near neighbors to our first white settlers. From the manuscript diary of David Godwin, a son of Captain Abraham Godwin, our pioneer inhabitant, we learn some surprisingly pleasant facts as to the intercourse and confidence existing between the lingering red men and the newcomers who were slowly but surely pushing them toward the setting sun. New Jersey has always been proud of the fact that not an acre of Indian land was ever taken from the original owners by force and without the payment of what was considered adequate compensation. And—with the exception of the so-called "Pavonia Massacres," at what is now Jersey City, in 1643 and 1654, brought about by the stupidity of the New Amsterdam Dutch under Governor Kieft—we can testify to the uniform kindliness and courtesy of the untutored children of the forest. These congenial traits were exhibited by the "savages" of New England in their dealings with the Plymouth colonists; and it is the concensus of opinion among modern historians as it was among the conscientious pathfinders of the eighteenth century, including Wm. Penn and Zinzendorf, that unscrupulous white men were responsible for most of the widely-exploited "savagery" of the aboriginal Americans. I am of the opinion, therefore, that what David Godwin has to say—and he writes from his own childhood experiences—will cause us to think of them in a more kindly retrospect:

> "Father had often to leave home for New York and to leave mother alone with her children, though I believe there were but two at that time. Their principal Chief, the only name I remember perfectly to hear my mother say, was Mashau. When he heard father had to leave home, he came over and told him to go, all would be safe, as he and another Chief would not leave the House until his return; which was strictly attended to. Father, to gain their confidence and make their lives agreeable, would when he had a Hogshead nearly empty of Rum put in some water with it and send for the Chief to take the Hogshead to their place to have a dance; but not let any harm arise from the effects of the Rum; which was strictly attended to. And when the frolick was over the Hogshead was carefully returned, filled with their work, such as trays, bowls, ladles, etc., worth ten times as much as all the Rum. In this way they lived happy for several years . . . About the time father commenced building over the river, the Indians

found their hunting ground got to be too public, and concluded to move back. The Chiefs went and selected a spot on the river at Menesinck where they moved, though the parting with them and the inhabitants was very hard. They had lived in the greatest harmony for years. The Chiefs would come down every spring and fall to Totowa and spend a week or fortnight with father and bring as much venison, young bears, and wild turkeys, and small game, as would last half of the inhabitants for a week. This they kept up for some time after; and while they were at Totowa whenever father went from home, they would not leave mother one hour alone. I have heard her say they would take my little brother with them to their Wigwam to play with their Papooses and return him in the evening loaded with their little trinkets, particularly with a little Papoose, perfectly ornamented with wampum and porcupine quills dyed in the most splendid colors."

It is not, however, curiosity as to how *modern* are the Indian trinkets and remains which we find, but how *ancient,* which leads us to speculate as to the age of these souvenirs. Dr. Charles Conrad Abbott, of Trenton, who in his "Ten Years' Digging in Lenape Land" and other delightful brochures, writes so entertainingly of primitive treasure-trove, loses all patience with us when we venture to broach this subject, and answers equivocally in a smoke-screen of petulance. He, having found skeletons and flints beneath the "glacial drift" along the banks of the lower Delaware, has become convinced, quite naturally, that man dwelt in the East Coast region before the devastating ice-cap put a period to human existence in these parts. I do not see why he should have become so cynical, and have lost his usual urbanity because he was asked "how long ago was this?" Admitted ignorance would have answered perfectly well.

This much I can say to those of inquiring mind

who like to delve into the dim recesses of times long past: Man has existed in America in some form or other, for fifty thousand years—more, most likely. This estimate is very conservative, in the light of modern scientific research. Read Henry Fairfield Osborn's works if you want science. I, alas, am most superficial, and like not either mental calisthenics or a delving into the profundities.

When one comes across a specimen of aboriginal handicraft which seems to be hoary with age, it may be classed as either weather or water-worn, patinated or calcined. The first classification implies that the fragment of worked stone has been exposed to the elements upon the ground for countless years or has suffered from the slow but sure abrasion of a running stream. Two hundred years mean nothing to a flint buried in undisturbed earth; but the same period of time might play great havoc with a point of poor material accidentally lost in the bed of a turbulent rivulet. "Patina" is a scientific word. It expresses a decomposition, beginning upon the surface and gradually working inward, to which even the "unchanging" rocks and hills are subject. Prof. Robert de Rustafjaell, famed for his Egyptian researches, whom I first met at Luxor in 1913, gave me some pre-dynastic flints, found at Kift in the Valley of the Nile, which showed a surface discoloration of perhaps 1/16 of an inch in depth, and which he surmised to be well upward of 25,000 years old. Allowing for the varying climatic conditions in dry Egypt and humid America, you may feel assured, if you find a decrepit-looking arrow point, which on being broken in twain shows a surface discoloration, that several millenniums have passed since the hand which fashioned it has turned to dust.

"Calcined," of course, refers to damage by fire. An arrow-point, trodden under a moccasined foot and inadvertently kicked into a fireplace, and in consequence subjected to repeated bakings, cannot endure the ordeal with equanimity. The result, of course, is an

ARROW AND SPEAR HEADS.

Large and broad points are usually spoken of as "spear-heads", although the characterization is a matter of opinion.

Beginning at the left:—"specimen one" illustrates a keenly pointed and perfect arrow-head of argillite found at Paterson: number two a badly weather-worn and aged point from Wallpack on the Delaware; the third a triangular point of black flint from Lake Macopin; the fourth a nicely barbed point of yellow jasper from Fairfield; (all of these places being in New Jersey) next a "leaf-shaped" specimen from Orange County, N. Y., and last a clumsy artifact of white quartz, minus the point, from the banks of the James River, Virginia. (This may have been a spear-head.)

Triangular tips, such as "number three" are commonly called "war points," because, having inflicted a wound they were not easily extracted. The shaft would pull out, of course, but the point had a tendency to remain embedded in the flesh.

ash-like surface. These specimens are occasionally met with on camp sites. They are interesting, but can prove no ancient lineage.

Acknowledging the fact that, with the introduction of firearms, the Indian gradually abandoned the bow and arrow, I think we are safe in saying that a neatly chipped and fresh-looking arrow point may range in age from two hundred to a thousand years; a calcined point must be an "unknown quantity"; and a patinated specimen may be literally "as old as the hills."

My solitary experience in the finding of a specimen of great and awesome antiquity came about in such a matter-of-fact way that I cannot resist the temptation to tell you the story. I am a lover of boys. Boys love the woods. In the attempt to induce a group of them to attend church occasionally I resorted to the "added and attractive inducement" of providing a shack in the country for their delectation. And we built ourselves a never-to-be-forgotten shelter.

"Locust Lodge" we facetiously called it; although nothing more than a temporary lean-to of small felled trees—subsequently expanded and excavated. In and around this rude structure were spent many delightful hours. It happened in the summer of 1921 and the succeeding fall and winter, this building of a little hut; and it was amid a five-acre grove of young locusts lying some seven miles north of Hackensack, N. J., between the old Paramus roadway and the Saddle River. One hundred feet back from the stream (the immediate banks of which are quite low-lying and subject to frequent inundation, but nevertheless heavily wooded with ancient oaks and beeches) a fifteen-foot rise in the terrain permitted an admirable site for our lodge. Between our selected spot and the busy roadway the thorny jungle of locusts afforded an ample barrier and well-nigh perfect seclusion. We swam in the river and fished to our hearts' content. Then came winter. Driven indoors, we began "digging in," and at night sang and cooked supper at the stone fireplace in the corner. (I suppose, for the amusement of those of my readers who love Nature, I should explain that a family of chipmunks found the interstices behind said fireplace a very comfortable home between the visits of my pirate crew, and scattered wrathfully whenever we kindled the fire, only to return when the embers had grown cold.)

In our "burrowing," we discovered that every foot of the surface loam yielded a multitude of chips, proof sufficient that we were not the original campers there. Beneath the alluvial deposit of perhaps a foot and a half of such soil as delights the farmer—evidence of long-ago floods on the part of a stream now quite circumspect—we found sand, reminiscent of the tranquil bed of an inter-glacial lake. And I, scraping industriously, with a trowel in one hand and a sandwich in the other, turned out one evening, by the firelight, a perfect arrow point, lying between the sand and the silt, buried far deeper than the plough had ever penetrated. The discovery of so venerable a specimen, under such circumstances, brings with it a singular thrill, far more stirring than the smug satisfaction which comes from the picking up of a "surface find" on a summer's day afield. The great fire of crackling logs; the warm-hearted boys, suddenly hushed in their trivial gossip, standing in a semi-circle of eager curiosity; the tiny bit of cold stone, so replete with human interest, resurrected from the oblivion of damp earth, telling a wordless story of the long, long past:—this picturesque combination of creature comfort, companionship and mental stimulus leaves little to be desired. Mariette, opening the long-hidden tombs of the Apis bulls at Sakkara, and beholding the footprints of ancient men upon its sand-strewn floor, experienced a feeling of awe no more profound than this little episode afforded us.

I think it was Dr. Talmadge who said: "mystery is written everywhere." And well it is for us; for things beyond our ken make us humble and reverent and open-minded. Realizing our own insignificance when it comes to matters of time and space and understanding, we lose ourselves in wonder; and in wonder we find the truth.

The old arrow-head has been thawing out these many weeks in the warmth of my library, and, although exceedingly reticent concerning its own long career, it seems to be taking something of an interest in the events of the new era. But for me it will always suggest the story of a far-distant yesterday. I can see in fancy some venturesome creature—hairy, strong-armed, and having semblance to a man—cautiously creeping northward in the path of the receding ice cap in quest of strange, uncanny prey—who trod these mysterious, lonely, perhaps dismal sands, and lost his aim and his arrow through a "flying shot" at a flitting thing which seemed "good to eat" in the days when Homer, or Pythagoras, or the Ayrians, were yet unborn!

CHAPTER II.

THE woodland tramper, having gone astray in an upland wilderness, with but an hour or two of remaining daylight, coming unexpectedly upon a tiny and musical rivulet, is instantly gladdened and reassured. By following its course, devious though it may be, he will eventually find a way out of the mysterious fastnesses of dark and dense forest, leading him to the cultivated lowlands and the haunts of men. Peradventure the gathering shadows may call for a halt and a bivouac for the night; but beside the stream he is no longer lost.

Both the moralist and the archaeologist may draw an analogy from mountain torrent and babbling brook. Let him who seeks the truth but catch in the murmuring voice of the waters the message that the great Creator of Nature is a *lover* of all mankind, and he has found the way, and found himself. The streamlet will lead him out from the shadows of doubt and fear into sunny fields of confidence and delight; his courage and usefulness will expand like the ever-widening river until, reaching the sea, and being bidden by the Great Spirit to tarry no longer, he is content to launch upon its bosom and put out toward unknown isles—sustained by a firm and abiding faith.

How wonderful a privilege it is, indeed, to walk beside the brook! And this business of finding oneself is such a rich experience. Quite recently, in conversation with a gentleman of wealth who has presented to one of our great Western cities an art gallery and a museum, I drew from him his conception of true philanthropy. To give to men and women a hitherto unseen vision of the beauty and breadth of life by enabling them to appropriate to themselves the spirit of the world's artists and sculptors as diffused through their masterpieces, is, in his opinion, a work well worthy of his untiring devotion. This is much in line with the thought expressed by the late Abram S. Hewitt, who always contended that the possession of means carried with it an obligation to mankind. Those of us who have a knowledge of books and pictures and Nature—the rudiments of self-confidence, vision and faith—owe to society a debt almost equal to that of those who are favored by the possession of a great store of material things. And we, having a faint concept of light and life, owe it to the multitudes of those who yet "dwell in darkness" to help them in the way of this same seeking and finding.

Have I indulged in "moralizing" to the postponement of my archaeology? I am sure of forgiveness, however, on the part of every rambler, for who can follow in the wooded paths trodden by a long-vanished people without becoming successively retrospective and introspective? And if he be a true man, he will desire for *others* the same peace of mind and capability for enjoyment which he himself has acquired.

The streams were well known and beloved by the first Americans. They followed their windings as the path of least resistance, and beside them built their wigwams. The shores of the upland lakes yield trifling things reminiscent of their erstwhile and long-continued habitation; and the bluffs beside the rolling ocean, as well as the great salt-water inlets, are found, almost without exception, to show traces of feast and council fire, of fishing and fowling, and sometimes of primitive warfare.

The boundaries of an existing lake or pond may not always be regarded as a reliable basis for exploration. Ascertain, first of all, whether or not such reservoirs are natural or the result of an artificial impounding of the waters. A five-foot dam at the outlet makes all the difference in the world; ancient shore lines are obliterated, and whatever there may be reminiscent of the quondam visitors, is hopelessly lost—unless some torrential freshet causes the retaining wall to give way. Should such a calamity occur in connection with a pond which you have reason to believe originally covered a more circumscribed area, make it your business to be on hand for the "first fruits" of the subsidence of the waters; for in this event the years of "washing" will have left the newly-exposed fringes of the prehistoric pond in prime condition for your purpose. Likely to be found are not only arrow heads, spear-points, and chips, but "net-sinkers" and those ever-possible rarities which undisturbed territory may hold in store.

The Indians, as fishermen, were subject to no game laws, but plied their vocation as suited their fancy. Thin and elongated flint points are often designated "fish-spears"; flint hooks, painstakingly fashioned, have been found at rare intervals, as well as occasional sharp, crooked bones, which it is conjectured have served a similar purpose; but the "net-sinker" is so unmistakable and typical as to be the ideal lake-side find. Flattened disks of stone, with fragments of the edges pecked away upon opposite sides, enabling them easily to be tied to the woven-grass meshes, are not at all exceptional, although sometimes spherical specimens with a shallow encircling groove seem to have been in favor. At Greenwood Lake, N. J. (the "Long Pond" of pre-Revolutionary days), I found one which was almost circular, a quarter of an inch in thickness, by perhaps two and a half in diameter, with indentations of a quarter of an inch.

Indian canoes constitute a subject worthy of an entire booklet, although few men would venture to handle it. Neither would they essay to handle the *canoes,* judging by the only one which I have seen. Of the "birch-barks" I know nothing. Surely a flat-footed, fat-paunched and clumsy savage would, perforce, handle such a craft with great discretion—or swim. My knowledge is confined to a solitary dug-out, found embedded in the mud of the meadows bordering on the Hackensack River and now preserved in a case at the museum of the Bergen County Historical Society at Hackensack, N. J. It is about sixteen feet in length by three in breadth of beam, at the widest; and was in all probability fashioned from a felled tree by means of stone axes and fire. The skill and workmanship of which primitive people were capable is strikingly displayed in the great war canoe from the South Sea Islands, now at the American Museum of Natural History, New York City. I am doubtful whether the North American Indian was called upon, by geographic circumstance, to develop boat-building to any such degree of perfection. Nevertheless, he could and did contrive boats which served

INDIAN FORDING PLACE
(Passaic River, West Paterson, N. J.)

Within a distance of some seven miles, the River Passaic, winding through the great Silk City of America, still preserves for us nine carefully constructed fords. The dams at Dundee and at the Great Falls have served to raise the normal water-level, and these aboriginal mementos would have been lost sight of, had not the demand for potable water to supply adjoining municipalities depleted the once ample flow of the Passaic. As it is, the shore lines of today do not differ materially from those of ancient times, and the fords give valuable clues as to the courses of several Indian trails which traversed this section of Northern New Jersey.

THE HUDSON RIVER, FROM THE PALISADES NEAR FORT LEE, N. J.

Without question, every mile of Hudson River waterfront would have yielded thousands of Indian artifacts and implements had there been a general and wide-spread interest in these things a century ago. Even today, despite the havoc wrought by the railways traversing both shores, there is much to be found in undisturbed nooks and corners at the base of the Palisades, and there are many tempting sites along the upper reaches of the great river which are accessible to the earnest explorer.

The situation here depicted is both historic and aboriginal in its associations. Across the stream is seen the upper portion of Manhattan Island, where stood Fort Washington in 1776. Near the spot from which the picture was taken were the river defences of Fort Lee. Between these two posts, the patriots undertook the construction of the first barrier to hostile shipping, the ineffectual "chevaux-de-frise." Both the New York and New Jersey shores, hereabout, have yielded their quota of Indian relics.

his purpose. For the wide Hudson he knew how to make a "sea-worthy" craft; but for the shallows of the inland waterways he found the light creations of bark and boughs to be much more appropriate.

We have no reason for supposing that the Indian, like the cat, was averse to wetting his feet; yet the numerous "fords" still existing (some of them having entailed the expenditure of much physical labor in their construction) attest to the fact that there were times at least when an immersion was not to his liking. In numberless instances, the troublesome rocks which have been concentrated in certain portions of the bed of a stream for the seeming purpose of impeding the progress of pleasure-seeking canoeists of today, are but the remains of carefully-arranged places of crossing.

In winter, quite naturally, a cold plunge was not to be regarded as an altogether pleasing experience. Hence a fording-place, provided by a chain of stones across rapids where no ice could form, was a decided luxury. Nor was it to be expected that every roving red-skin carried a canoe. The necessity for the fords, therefore, is quite obvious. They are more common than might be supposed by one unfamiliar with Indian usage. Thickly-strewn bowlders of varying sizes, placed in a V or W arrangement across the shallow portions of rivers, with the "points" downstream, are invariably the foot-bridges of the aborigines. They sometimes served a double purpose. If, at the extremity of the angle an opening was left, it was used as a "weir" or fish-trap. The Indians were adept in the fashioning of seines or nets, and had no scruples about beating the stream, commencing many yards above the "catch-all" and advancing in phalanx formation toward the barrier, driving into the net those luckless members of the finny tribe which failed to sense the impending danger and make their escape by swimming against the current between the muscular limbs of their cunning enemies.

Cataracts seem to have possessed a peculiar charm for the red men, and those exceptional in depth of fall or in volume of overflow were regarded with something akin to awe and reverence. Even we ourselves, although sophisticated and hardened by the experiences of modern life, are not proof against the spell of falling waters. Niagara, justly famed for its majestic beauty, is in truth and similitude the fountain-head of inspiration for him who is a lover of Indian lore. Viewed from the supposedly less advantageous point upon the American shore of the gorge, near the monument commemorating Father Hennepin the path-finder, it is the place of all most desirable for meditation and communion with those legendary figures whom we have been following through forest and stream. The appended picture was taken in some such spirit of retrospect, from an angle which obscured anything bearing semblance to the "progress of the twentieth century." Here we have a dim suggestion of the great gulf, unmarred by power-generating stations, groups of tourists, or even the heroic little "Maid of the Mist." Thus must the falls have appeared to Pontiac and Brant, and the last of the Mohicans. As to whether or not traces of the Indians have been found in the neighborhood of Niagara, I cannot say from personal experience. May I be permitted, however, to digress for a moment and make one or two upper New York State observations which may not be out of order.

In the Onondaga County Court House at Syracuse, N. Y., there is a striking mural painting by William De L. Dodge portraying "Hiawatha, the Legendary Genius of the Onondagas." My reproduction gives but a poor conception of its powerful

NIAGARA

In the thunder of Niagara's fall we hear the whispering voice of the Creator. John L. Stoddard, than whom no speaker was more eloquent, failed to find words of his own with which to describe its sublime majesty, and turned to Charles Dickens for an adequate avenue of expression. The latter, in recounting his American experiences, thus speaks of the stupendous cataract:

"It was not till I came to Table Rock—that it all flashed upon me in its might and majesty. Then, when I felt how near to my Creator I was standing, the first impression and the lasting one of this tremendous spectacle was—PEACE; calm recollections of the Dead, great thoughts of an eternal rest and happiness!"

"HIAWATHA"
The Legendary Genius of the Onondagas

Beautifully has Dodge, the great mural painter, depicted the spirit of the Indian in this colorful masterpiece in the Syracuse (N. Y.) Court House. Ever since the ancient Greeks and Romans employed this branch of decorative art to embellish the stone walls of their villas, the lovers of the beautiful have realized the possibilities of great blank surfaces. In the Public Library at Boston, Abbey and Sargent have similarly labored with wonderful results. In the Pantheon at Paris and in the Congressional Library at Washington we find the same opportunities improved to delightful advantage.

The American Indian seems not to have been adept in the business of pictorial decoration. Save to bedaub his own oily hide with ochre, indigo and the red juice of berries, he made little use of pigment. Rarely indeed have aboriginal traces of portraiture or modeling been discovered.

appeal. It seems to say to those who come to the busy county seat to record conveyances and mortgages (all concerning lands which were once the undisputed property of a powerful Indian nation)—"Keep the whole earth if you want it, may it give you happiness; as for me, I go to the land where the Great Spirit dwells!" In the tale of Hiawatha, Longfellow permits his hero to make a graceful exit; but this picture conveys the idea of a more dramatic climax. The birch canoe has seemingly entered the rapids. The lone paddler, having vainly tried to stem the current and make the shore, has yielded to the inevitable. We may conjecture as to the end.

Indeed, if sentiment is to be indulged in, it were better to think of a vanished race of noble and heroic red men, than to visit some of the Eastern "reservations" where, under Government protection, the remnants of the Six Nations dwell today. Garbed in a pathetic mixture of the shabby and ill-fitting clothes of the white men, in a wretchedness and squalor accentuated by a few beads and feathers reminiscent of departed glory, they are a sorry-looking crew. Those among them who determine to mingle with the conquerors and share in the conquest, seldom fail to achieve success in true American fashion; but those who are content to remain as indolent almoners are like the dead fish which float downstream. In the West, of course, the story is different.

Among the "secondary" cataracts, I believe the falls of the Passaic at Paterson, N. J., is the most attractive. In common with the more stupendous Niagara, it has many traditions, associated with the primitive people by whom it was known and loved, and who frequented its rocky chasm. Most popular, of course, among the folk-lore of the Indians, were the stories of half-fabulous heroes and heroines who, in the very long ago, permitted themselves to be dashed over these watery precipices thereby to appease the Higher Power, or in expiation of some fancied transgression. These self-sacrificing scapegoats came in for much posthumous adulation, I suppose, and maybe are now among the "elect." But "obedience was ever more efficacious than sacrifice" (to paraphrase the Scriptures) and—be it recorded to their credit—the great majority of the red-skins, while stoics by nature, were withal eminently practical, and spectacular suicides were unpopular.

INDIAN DUG-OUT CANOE
In the Museum of the Bergen County Historical Society, Hackensack, N. J.

This is the unique specimen of Indian boat-building to which reference is made on page 22 of the text. It was unearthed in 1868 near the Hackensack River, on the property of Judge Garret G. Ackerson, Hudson Street. The United States Forestry Department has identified the wood as white oak.

Water falls were, however, usually associated with such naturally favored camp sites as to be resorted to for purely utilitarian reasons. Sheltering rocks contiguous to good water, especially-commanding elevations, and in fact any unusual topographical oddities varying an otherwise "tame" countryside, are seldom to be found devoid of traces of prehistoric man. Particularly is this the case if, in bygone days, there were nearby marshes suitable for fishing or fowling.

The Passaic Falls, according to the accounts handed down by the founders of Paterson, were well known and often visited by the Indians. Several fine "rock-shelters" used to exist in the valley below the basin, where the foaming waters readjusted themselves for a more tranquil passage to the sea, before the despoiling hand of man saw fit to fill them in with dirt and debris. Archaeologically, the site has now been hopelessly ruined. The fact remains, notwithstanding, that these falls were once upon a time (what the falls in *your* native town may prove to be) an erstwhile rendezvous of the Indians and an exceptional field for endeavor. Bestir yourselves, then, before the opportunity is gone forever, remembering that what is true of great and imposing waterfalls is applicable, in reasonable measure, to every picturesque tumbling cascade having a suitable camp-site nearby.

Without some mention of Indian shell-heaps, my observations on water-front sites would be incomplete. Very many far-inland camping places have yielded a few oyster and clam shells, attesting to the fact that occasional supplies of crustaceous delicacies penetrated into the interior, carried thither, most likely, by traveling natives from the coast, and bartered for upland commodities. From other favored aboriginal resorts near mountain water courses come many long-buried unio shells, the housings of the so-called fresh water mussels, which seem to have been a popular article of diet among the red men. Indeed, there are many shallow places in the Passaic and Saddle rivers and the Notch Brook (all in upper New Jersey) where you will find an abundance of these living shell-fish today, and I suppose this holds true in hundreds of other streams unbeknown to me. It is a source of much relaxation, while on a canoeing excursion, to gather a dozen or so of these bivalves and open them up in search of fresh-water pearls. At intervals some one discovers a gem of considerable value, and then a general hunt is inaugurated, resulting in a promiscuous slaughter of the innocents. I know of no one, however, who has attempted to eat these mussels, except one of my boys at camp—who pronounced them tough and unpalatable—and the more-appreciative muskrats. In proof of this last statement I have seen many piles of emptied shells beneath the water near much-frequented muskrat holes in river banks. I think the energetic rodents carry on this work during the shut-in months of winter, swimming beneath the ice and scouring the creek bottoms for a considerable distance in quest of this "tasty" food. As to the finding of pearls (formed after the manner of Nature in ocean depths) some years seem to be more favorable than others. During eight or nine seasons I found none whatever; in 1922, out of some twenty specimens which I essayed to pry open with a jack-knife, I found two small ones. I am something of a sentimentalist, however, and it seems wasteful and sacrilegious to destroy life, even of so low an organism, without a legitimate excuse. If one were on the verge of starvation, I doubt not that the shells, well roasted in the embers, would provide a fairly satisfactory meal; but in these days when an excess of scientific knowledge has made us wary of ptomaines, germs and microbes, we are too fastidious, I fear.

The true "shell-heap" is quite different from a camp-site where, in the blackened earth, we find occasional shells such as those of which I have spoken. Seashore shell-deposits are a worthy field of study in themselves. Under these circumstances the excavator finds himself delving into a veritable stratum of shells, *with black dirt interspersing the shells, rather than occasional shells buried in the earth.* Some of the bulletins of the American Museum of Natural History treat the subject scientifically; my personal experience embraces but two expeditions, the first of which was an unsought adventure. In 1919, while en

THE FALLS OF THE PASSAIC
(Paterson, N. J.)

Paterson owes the circumstance of its founding, as well as its steady commercial development, to the "great falls." In 1780 Alexander Hamilton, acting as one of Washington's aides, first saw the cataract. Impressed by its wonderful water-power possibilities, he was impelled, a dozen years later, to assist in founding the "Society for the Establishment of Useful Manufactures" with a view to the utilization of this vast natural resource of energy. Major L' Enfant, (afterward famed for his work in connection with the new Capital City of Washington) laid out Paterson's original plan of sluiceways and mill races, some of which are in use today. Ever-increasing demands for potable water have reduced the volume of the Passaic River; and the diversion of the remaining supply to operate a giant turbine power-plant (which now generates electrical energy), leaves the once famous cataract, at times, entirely destitute; but the chasm remains as a reminder of a bygone beauty.

THE BRONX RIVER
WHITE PLAINS, N. Y.

Aside from its historic associations, in that Washington threw his army behind this little streamlet in 1776, during the maneuvers in Westchester County—the Bronx River upholds the tradition that the aboriginal trails adhered closely to the winding waterways. Local enthusiasts can produce many a choice specimen of Indian skill in implement-making, found along the borders of the Bronx. High banks, similar to the knoll above the bridge, will usually be found to be favored sites. If cuttings have recently been made in such hillocks, exposing the strata of the embankment, a close examination of the arable "top layer" of earth is to be recommended. Every shower dislodges chips and pebbles from the "culture level", and exposes tell-tale clues. Patches of earth from which the sod has been cut are likewise promising at all times.

route to Pope's Creek, Virginia, to visit the birthplace of Washington, I became stranded for the night at Pope's Creek, *Maryland,* on the River Potomac. In the early hours of the morning following, while waiting for the mail-boat, I discovered that many acres of the land contiguous to the river were thickly overlaid with shells. In one spot, where a wagon-road had been cut through an embankment, the shell deposit appeared to have a thickness of at least four feet. It is astounding to contemplate the number of years required to build up such an accumulation of refuse. Countless feasts must have been held here centuries before the coming of the Cavalier settlers, for these heaps of shells represent oft-repeated and sumptuous repasts; routine, I suppose, for the coastal Indians, but rare treats for such visiting braves of the mountains and of the Ohio who may have come, on occasion, to meet in council with their painted brethren of the seaboard. Frankly admitting that I found nothing in the way of relics among these shells by the wide and beautiful Potomac, I say without reservation that the experience will never be forgotten, for it proved to me that the Indians were not infrequent prowlers in these romantic regions, but that it was their age-old homeland. Powhattan and Pocahontas were not aliens. This was indeed *their country,* and had been peopled by their very numerous forebears, in great numbers, for a period so long that even our learned anthropologists are non-committal.

More positive deductions resulted from two visits to Indian feasting grounds nearer home. I refer to the shell heaps on the uppermost extremity of Manhattan Island, in a locality known as Inwood. To the uninitiated it may seem astounding to be informed that within ten minutes of busy Broadway, where it is intersected by Dyckman Street, there yet remain a few acres of undisturbed Nature, a bit of well-nigh virgin forest, rich in aboriginal associations. Yet such is the case. And here, bordering the Harlem Ship Canal (the old-time Spuyten Duyvil Creek), will be found an ancient tree, far more aged than any of its companions, whose observations have covered two and a half centuries. Historically, the neighborhood is interesting, because in the adjacent waters the hard-pressed Americans fitted out their "fire ships" in 1776, thereby to wreak vengeance upon the invading British vessels anchored some miles up the nearby Hudson. Archaeologically, it offers for us the most extensive bed of shell deposits in all the region 'round.

Behind the numerous boat houses, which are scattered along the Harlem River at this point, the dense forest—haunted by memories of long-vanished and savage denizens—still defies the despoiling hand of civilization. So numerous and widely distributed are the shell pits, that the locality is conjectured to have been a communal rendezvous for the widely scattered tribes of the Manhatta. Around the council-fires kindled at this spot the red men may have held friendly intercourse with the earliest traders, with whom they appear to have been extremely cordial, once having conquered their first and by no means groundless fears. The giant tulip tree at Inwood has been carefully "surgeoned" and around it a neat iron fence has been erected. The inscription which has been lettered upon the surface of one of its cement "fillings" gives not only the approximate age of the arboreal patriarch, but informs the visitor that the neighborhood was, in all likelihood, the site of one of Hendrick Hudson's interviews with the natives.

The shell deposits in themselves are a never-failing source of delight for one who is temperamentally adapted to patient seeking and is, by the lure of prob-

THE ANCIENT TULIP TREE AT INWOOD
(Manhattan Island—New York City)

Beneath and around which the ground is thickly overlaid with deposits of oyster and clam shells, attesting to the popularity of this river-side resort.

THE FALLS OF THE YOUGHIOGHENY

(Ohio Pyle, Fayette Co., Penna.)

The Indians of western Pennsylvania have made for themselves a reputation in American history which is by no means enviable. For this, however, the English and French were responsible. Striving for supremacy as they were, and bitter antagonists, the rival colonists made tools of the hapless redskins who dwelt in the coveted territory. The latter, realizing that they themselves would be the ultimate losers, had no scruples as to a little indiscriminate scalping and plundering when opportunity offered.

The beautiful scenery of the Laurel Hills, (of which the above bit of waterfall is typical;) the rugged grandeur of Pike County, in the opposite corner of the state; and the solitudes of the wild Lycoming Valley; suggest a world of possibility to him who seeks "unexplored" Indian stamping grounds.

able "finds," inclined to get down on his hands and knees and devote occasional hours to burrowing. While traces of much desultory digging are everywhere apparent, the transient visitor will have no difficulty in finding an undisturbed spot. Let him, therefore, carefully remove the low-lying tendrils of some aged vine, and, pushing aside the dead leaves of many autumns, begin to scratch about, wood-chuck fashion, in his own "unexplored" shell-patch. While he will be extremely unlikely to find jewel-encrusted sceptres or embalmed remains, the stray potsherd, crude stone "scraper," or broken spear-head of flint which is sure to reward him (if he has sufficient persistence) will more than compensate for knee-worn trousers and an aching back. Prof. Schliemann, who excavated some of the grand ruins of ancient Greece, was made no happier by his discoveries than you will be by some tiny relic of long-forgotten days. When your afternoon's work is done and you come back through the prosaic city of the present with your little treasures of the past tucked in your vest pocket, your own innermost soul will tell you that you are infinitely the gainer by the adventure you have enjoyed in the "world apart." If you are a novice you will be strongly tempted to engage in conversation with the man who sits beside you in the subway and to show him what you have found. But those of us who have older grown know how idle it is to expect a stranger to "respond" with an enthusiasm equal to our own. From experience, we realize that an impassable gulf divides the man whose soul aspires, from him who is matter-of-fact and essentially practical. Nine chances out of ten, your fellow passenger would fail to comprehend. By what possibility could a humble arrow-head mean anything to the man who sells cloaks and suits, underpays his hirelings, collects rents from tenement dwellers, lends money at usurious rates, and forecloses chattel-mortgages upon delinquent debtors? Within the heart of "*one* among ten," nevertheless, as in the story of the lepers healed by the Master of Men, some spirit of understanding may be found. In the ranks of this "tenth-man brotherhood," stand the men of all ages who are grateful for the chance to live and serve, who know full well how to toil, but possess withal that spirit of comprehension, which makes them worthy to "have dominion over the earth."

DOMESTIC UTENSILS
Indian Corn bowl and Pestle, with pitted Hand-hammer. The specimen at the left is a smoothed blue-stone Celt.

CHAPTER III.

WE of the present day cherish vague ideas as to the appearance and character of the Indians. Before we began to know them archaeologically, they seemed to us only vengeful and cunning savages, ever on the war path. Then, as we found a few pathetic remains of their sojourn here and there, we thought of them less harshly; for indeed it were difficult to think ill of a people who fished and hunted and struggled for an existence, with little or nothing to be gotten out of life but the most primitive creature comforts. Of course, no one now living remembers these dwellers along the Atlantic seaboard. True enough, we have ourselves encountered very aged persons whose grand parents told them "first-hand" stories of an occasional half-civilized red-skin who once again visited the haunts of his fathers, but these second-childhood reminiscences count for very little I am sure. It is to be regretted that more of our pioneers did not follow the example of David Godwin and set down contemporary memoirs. I suppose they little thought then that we should care to know. Quite recently, in connection with certain private research work for one of our old and respected families, I received from Europe copies of a number of eighteenth century letters written by one Peter Hasenclever, a German merchant who came to America in 1764 on behalf of a syndicate of London capitalists, and who had charge of the iron mines at Ringwood, N. J., and large agricultural enterprises in New York Province. This gentleman, a man of affairs, who knew the world from extensive traveling in many lands, has much to say regarding colonial America. From a communication to a friend in the homeland dated Aug. 16th, 1765, I quote the following, being fully assured that—while the facts set forth may be commonplace—these particular "side-lights" on our aboriginal friends have never before appeared in English:

> "Certain it is that the native Americans are, on the whole, weaker than the Europeans. Yet they are of medium height and their food and mode of life do not permit them to become stout. They dwell in the woods, roaming about constantly and subsisting almost entirely on the chase. Occasionally, they have more food than necessary, but for the most part they suffer the pangs of hunger. Of vegetables they use mostly Indian corn or maize, planted and harvested by the women. Pounded in a wooden mortar, they make of it a sort of mush. If the harvest miscarries, as sometimes happens, their misery is great. In winter they live on smoked meat of deer, bear, or beaver. Nor is hunting always good. Yet they are frugal and quite inured to famine. The men only go on the chase, while the women do all kinds of domestic chores. If the man shoots a bear or deer near his hut, his wife must drag it home; all he does is to blaze the way to it by breaking off twigs.
> Whenever the family moves from one place to another, the

women are compelled to carry the baggage, blankets, kettles, etc. Babies are placed on top of the bundle, and when not yet weaned, they are wrapped up in mattings and fastened to a small board. When squatting down in the woods or building a fire, they place board and child against a tree or suspend it from a branch as a precaution against snakes; and, in this position, with the wind blowing, it is likely to swing to and fro. Often I was amazed to see the small creatures on the backs of their mothers, with the sun glaring in their face or the rain running into their eyes, and yet they never cried.

The hovels, which they build here and there on their wanderings, are wretched. They consist of bark, peeled off the trees and spread out over poles in such a way that the water can run off. But in their settlements, which are made up of several families, the wigwams or huts are comfortable enough. As a rule, they are circular, with a fireplace in the centre, and directly above is a hole in the roof for the smoke to escape. Round about the fire are their couches of bear, beaver or other skins. This peltry improves after they have slept on it through the winter.

In point of moderation and charity they certainly set an example to civilized peoples. When the savage has something, he divides it in equal parts with his family and friends; even an apple he will cut up in six or more portions, if there be so many persons present.

They talk very little among themselves; they have few subjects which they might discuss, and for this reason their language is not rich in words: for their work and occupation consists almost wholly in hunting and fishing. Their way of expressing anything is usually allegorical, and in this manner they will make their meaning very clear."

In these few paragraphs, the observant writer has said a great deal. If his word-pictures of Indian life are not of sufficient realism, let me suggest that, when next you visit New York City, you spend an afternoon at the American Museum of Natural History. Besides a superbly-arranged collection of implements and pottery, there are a number of wonderful life-size groups portraying aboriginal family life. The finely-executed wax figures are incomparably superior to anything I have seen along this line, modeled upon a scientific basis by men who are not only artists but anthropologists. Peter Hasenclever's characterization of the constantly toiling Indian woman is here recreated most delightfully in a squat, flat-nosed squaw whose face you will like to remember, for it is not at all repulsive (although maybe "unlovely" from our point of view). The squaws were, I fear, the actual workers among the Indian people; and chief among their implements of labor were the hoe, the mortar and pestle, and the pitted "hand-hammer."

Indian stone hoes are among the rarest of finds. They are difficult of description because of the great variety of shapes (often being merely crude flat stones) which the red-skins contrived to fasten to a stick. I think the employment of stones for this purpose was less common than the use of thick tortoise shells, or fire-toughened briar roots with one of the stalks utilized for a handle. In the case of these shell or wooden implements, there is nothing left to be found by the searcher of today. The hoes I have seen are, for the most part, nearly triangular in shape, and are sometimes notched, resembling the adze to a degree. Often, in browsing about in an Indian field, we come across a stone which we conjecture to have served this purpose, but lacking any trace of human elaboration, and showing no evidence of chipping or abrasion on the broad edge, we regretfully discard it; because mere speculation does not make a specimen. If fashioned from a thin slab, hoes sometimes show one or more perforations, the holes being carefully drilled and

HALF-WAY UP THE PALISADES
(Sneden's Landing, Rockland Co., N. Y.)

For eighteen miles the famous Palisades flank the west bank of the Hudson with a wall so precipitous that, in many places, the ascent is practically impossible. It is the logical conclusion that the few available "landings" of today are identical with the natural rifts where ancient trails began and ended—where the red wanderers, coming down from the highlands by way of Tappan, beheld their beloved river and descended to its shores.

At such a storied spot, midway between the summit and the water-front, stands this ancient stone cottage, occupying what must have been a favored camp-site of the Indians. It has been artistically remodeled, and its quaint garden of other days transformed into a little paradise of rose-covered bowers.

Across the river is Dobbs Ferry. Many times each day, during the months of open navigation, a weather-beaten launch braves the intervening mile of wind-tossed water, piloted by an heroic old skipper who endeavors to make connections with all east-shore trains.

INDIAN CORN-BOWLS OR "MORTARS," PRESERVED AT RINGWOOD MANOR

(Passaic Co., N. J.)

At the base of several of the arboreal giants adorning the lovely grounds of Ringwood Manor have been placed the ancient Indian grinding bowls which have been found upon the estate. Filled with water, as they usually are, they appeal strongly to the birds of the neighborhood as appropriate bathing pools.

The site of the Manor House, occupying that of the home of Robert Erskine, the Revolutionary master of the mines, was undoubtedly a favored rendezvous of the Indians because of its commanding position at the bend of Ringwood River. Beholding its natural beauties from the shaded veranda, one calls to mind the picturesque excerpt from the oration of Charles Sprague, the "banker poet," delivered at Boston in 1825:

"Not many generations ago, where you now sit, circled with all that exalts and embellishes civilized life, the rank thistle nodded in the wind, and the wild fox dug his hole unscared. Here lived and loved another race of beings. Beneath the same sun that rolls over your heads, the Indian hunter pursued the panting deer; gazing on the same moon that smiles for you, the Indian lover wooed his dusky mate."

"counter-sunk." It appears that sand, water, and infinite labor were the essentials to this tiresome operation, and the specimens usually show that the drilling was done from both sides. Sometimes Nature, by thoughtfully providing slight pits or defects in the stone, gave the patient artisan an encouraging start. While at times the edges of hoes have been sharpened by "chipping," they belong on the whole to the class of implements which might be called "smoothed," in that—unlike the flints with keen and crisp edges—their worked surfaces, and usually the entire specimen, have been rubbed to a fairly even surface.

Indian pestles resemble those used by the modern druggist or color maker in grinding powders and pigments; while the mortars or bowls of the aboriginal people answered the same purpose as those employed today. Pestles (either perfect stones of cylindrical shape, or fragments thereof) are quite common. As a rule they were long, thin and club-shaped, gradually brought to a more symmetrical form either by design or long-continued use. The material is likely to be anything *except* flint or slate. Hard granite-like stones, picked from heaps of glacial morain and exotic in character, was often availed of. As to the receptacles almost universally spoken of as "corn-bowls," they vary greatly in character. Sometimes wood was employed; one specimen found in Passaic County is made of the gnarled wood of the apple tree, and is wonderfully preserved. Some of the stone bowls were beautifully wrought, and of such excellent material that they surely must have been communal or family heirlooms of great antiquity, the loss or fracture of which would have brought tears to the proverbially dry eyes of the most stoical savage. Others, found in the neighborhood of village sites, are nothing more than small bowlders with a natural surface depression, donated by mother Nature for the use of her industrious daughters. Still more ponderous fragments of rock—similarly formed—which never could be removed from the place where they were deposited aeons ago, remained as fixtures; and these are often met with in frequently-visited mountain retreats, and appear to have been utilized repeatedly by transient or migratory bands.

The hand-hammer is a flat, round stone, shaped like a cake, perhaps an inch or two in thickness; such a stone as the boys would call a "scaler." The difference between the valueless millions of similar stones which are everywhere to be found, and the few which are somewhere awaiting a place in your collection, is but a matter of two slight "pits" or hollows (one on either face of the "cookie"). These tell-tale concavities of no great depth mean that the specimen so branded was one of the handiest and most popular of the implements utilized in the "domestic science" of the Indian housewife. Grasped between the thumb and one of the fingers it was the family nut-cracker—or maybe it cracked hot bones from the fire for the sake of the succulent marrow—at any rate it cracked to good purpose.

I suppose I ought to say something (while upon the subject of rubbed and polished implements) about the tomahawk and the hatchet—now, by reason of their scarcity, considered the most highly to be desired of all aboriginal curios. The finding of one's first *arrow-head* as we have said, is a never-to-be-forgotten experience; but the discovery of the *first tomahawk* is an epoch-making adventure. I envy anyone who lives in a region which has not been "fine-combed" for these things. Hereabout, as everywhere, I imagine, the early farmers came in for the choice "pickings." Now as to tomahawk-hunting in the Eastern States, there are but two or three lanes of possibility. First and foremost comes the farmer's "stone fence."

Heaven forbid that I should be the cause of vandalism perpetrated upon those time-honored boundaries erected between fields by the honest settlers; yet the fact remains that these elongated landmarks have within them many a relic of the Indians. Of course, the building of a stone fence was a distinctly utilitarian measure, ridding the land to be enclosed of its great pebbles and at the same time constituting a barrier which, if well put together, might be expected to last indefinitely. Now, as those who built the fences were by no means as keenly interested in tomahawks and pestles and hammers as are you and I, and to them, as a rule, "a stone was a stone," the case is a clear one. But not so the fence. Admitting that it is neither scientific nor gentlemanly nor safe to pull them down—with emphasis on the modern spirit of "safety first" (as many farmers do not discriminate between a "scientist" gathering "data" and a small boy gathering apples, when it comes to administering a load of buckshot)—my advice is to carefully scrutinize all the aforesaid fences you pass and let your conscience be your guide.

Of course there are always the surprising "occasional finds" which come when least expected. I doubt the wisdom of constantly looking toward the ground when indulging in rambles or when walking the city streets, although you may thereby find an arrow-head or ten-cent piece, depending upon where you happen to be. He whose mind is on the ground alone misses much of Nature's overhead glory. In this matter, as in all else, the golden medium is to be sought. There is no need for stooping nor stumbling, nor falling over backward; but one can train one's eye to be well-nigh all-observant. Watch the wild creatures, and see how well they put this into practice.

Tomahawks have been found in un-looked-for places; in crystal trout pools, on the banks of lakes and rivers, or beneath some of those wonderful sheltering rocks beloved of the red wanderer, of which we shall speak in greater detail after a while, and which, when discovered, are more likely to be found undisturbed than any other of his typical haunts. If, despite all your searching, fortune fails to reward you in the quest for a specimen of the Indian's "weapon of persuasion," you may be able to induce some good-natured farmer to exchange one for a box of cigars. As to their actual money value, a man with a hundred two-dollar bills could, if he made sufficient inquiry and devoted a month to the quest, buy a hundred stone axes. But it is, of course, by far more fun to *find* one.

The distinction between axes, tomahawks and celts ought to be explained. The axe may be considered as a heavy tomahawk. The tomahawk is usually a light-weight and rather shapely axe. They may be likened to buxom and slender children of the same parentage. The celt is a modified form of the tomahawk, but was used rather as a chisel or—on occasion —as a skinning knife. Perhaps, in making plain the points of radical difference between the three, the chapter-heading illustrations will help, although specimens vary greatly, many of them having features showing a resemblance to their adamantine cousins. Adamantine were these ancient and chunky axes, assuredly; and one wonders how, in the name of all goodness, they were ever sharpened and grooved so nicely. The object of the lateral groove was, of course, to permit the split handle to encircle and bind the implement. From experiments I have made in the matter of

A ROCK SHELTER WHICH YIELDED NO RELICS
"Tory Rock" (between Echo Lake and Midvale, N. J.)

Some excursions to the supposed haunts of the Indians are bound to have negligible results so far as archaeological yield, notwithstanding which they resolve themselves into delightful woodland rambles. Such a reward characterized a visit to "Tory Rock" amid the southern spurs of the Ramapo Mountains, which owes its name to the fact that, during a period of the Revolution, it sheltered Royalist refugees and deserters from both armies. Here the renegade band is supposed to have dwelt in a perfect spirit of unanimity, sustaining themselves by occasional hunting and frequent forays upon the outlying farms.

The heaped up and riven bowlders form quite an extensive cavern, but its floor is of so rocky and uneven a character as to preclude the accumulation of relic-bearing earth. This habitation, therefore, was entirely devoid of Indian remains, and traces of its former occupancy by white men were likewise conspicuous by their absence.

AGED ELM AT HOHOKUS
(Bergen County, N. J.)

This venerable tree, the last living acquaintance of the Indians in this vicinity, stands beside the road from Paramus to Hohokus, having witnessed the passing of full two centuries and survived its youthful comrades by many years. The shadow of Mr. Schrabisch falls upon the memorial tablet which reminds the passer-by that this is the identical highway traversed many times by Washington while en route from the Hudson to the Ramapo. Then, I presume, it was a narrow country road; now, in order to permit its widening as befits a part of the improved interstate highway, it has been deemed necessary to encroach upon the roots of the tree itself. Quite recently, a violent storm played havoc with its northern branches, so today, while still very much alive, the tree has been curtailed at both ends, and evidently experiences sensations of deep humiliation.

fashioning wooden handles for the axes and tomahawks in my collection, I prefer a willowy stick, the binding end of which may be pared down to a narrow and supple band, which after tightly embracing the weapon, is returned again to the handle and tied with a thong. Unless a naturally forked stick was employed for the other mode, I find it difficult to determine how a sufficiently tight grip upon the stone head was obtained. Some years ago a stone axe was found upon the bottom of a pond at Thorndale, Dutchess County, N. Y., with its original wooden handle. This specimen illustrated another method of fastening—perhaps the best among the several expedients to which the Indians resorted for this purpose. It was evident that the stone implement had been forced into a notch cut through a very young and rapidly-growing sapling, to which (after a period of many months) the ingenious savages returned to reclaim the prize. As expected, the vigorous tree had, during the interval, tightened itself about the axe-head to the perfect satisfaction of the red-skins; a first-class weapon was theirs for the taking, and no great harm had been done—for the loss of one small tree meant little to bounteous Nature. Chief among the desirable characteristics of the true axe were weight, thickness and cutting edge. Months of patient rubbing must have been lavished upon some of the beautiful museum pieces I have seen, whereas others are clearly the hasty creations of necessity, with no pretense of cutting edge, being mauls rather than axes. Perhaps these were intended for war-clubs; in which event one blow would have proved for the luckless victim an adequate passport to the Happy Hunting Grounds.

As the "dress-sword" of colonial days differed from the sabre of the dragoon, so the prettily-formed tomahawk was perhaps more of a ceremonial "side-arm" than the rugged axe. At any rate, when the traders sought to provide an article thoroughly to the liking of their prospective customers, they imported a shapely iron. hatchet fashioned along similar lines. Only rarely have any of these "trade-hatchets" been found on Indian sites, for the reason, most likely, that the departing braves prized them too highly to leave them behind. The stone weapons of their fathers, having given place to the flintlocks of the whites, might well be left to rest in the blackened earth where they had chanced to fall, or in the corner of some sheltering hillside cairn to which they would come no more; but the precious blankets, arms and trinkets of the invaders which had corrupted their primitive simplicity were now the most treasured among the meagre possessions with which they began life anew as they returned once again to the West from which they had come.

The chisel-like celts, taken collectively, show a remarkable perfection of symmetry and workmanship. In common with tomahawks and axes, they belong to the class of smoothed and polished artifacts. Quite often the entire surface was polished, although the cutting edge received the most attention. Dr. C. C. Abbott, keen student of the subject though he was, admits that the use to which they were put is now a matter of speculation. In a meadow contiguous to Greenwood Lake, N. J., I found a specimen—lying exposed upon the surface of the ground—of beautifully smoothed bluestone, with beveled edges, in texture of material not unlike the enduring "blue" tombstones to be found in old New England graveyards. The upper end of the celt was rounded, and was certainly never intended by the maker to be pounded upon, although in other respects, it would have served admirably as a wedge or gouge. If employed as a skinning knife, however (supposing the actual incisions to have been made with a sharp flint blade) my specimen would have proved a perfect instrument—its narrow "top edge" quite effective for work upon such pelts as would have been ruined by a puncture, but must perforce be separated from the carcasses of their late owners before they could cover the broad shoulders of the huntsmen.

Some authorities like to imagine the "celt" as having been used as a gouge, and thus, as an adjunct to fire, being an efficient aid in the hollowing and shaping of log canoes or dug-outs. But clam-shells would have answered equally well for this operation. My own opinion of the celt is that it was a light and handy tool employed for purposes "too numerous to mention" for the good and sufficient reason that we do not begin to know them.

Here and there in this fragmentary monograph reference is made to "scrapers." Any fragment of stone with one or more intentionally sharpened edges may be thus denominated. They were used for numerous domestic purposes such as the removal of grease from earthen pots or tortoise-shell platters, the dressing of hides and the like. The so-called "sinew-dresser" was a stone in which was a cut or groove through which thongs of hide or gut were passed to reduce them to a uniform and usable degree of thinness.

Migratory as the Indians were, they invariably traveled afoot. Nature having given them no camels, elephants, nor oxen, the women were called upon to bear the burdens. To the best of our knowledge, the horse was a European importation. His American descendant, the mustang, has proven a patient, faithful and long-suffering companion to the picturesque nomad of the Western plains; but the East-coast Algonquin was forced to depend upon the "ladies" of his family when moving day came 'round. Being monogamous is practice, and the carrying capacity of one poor

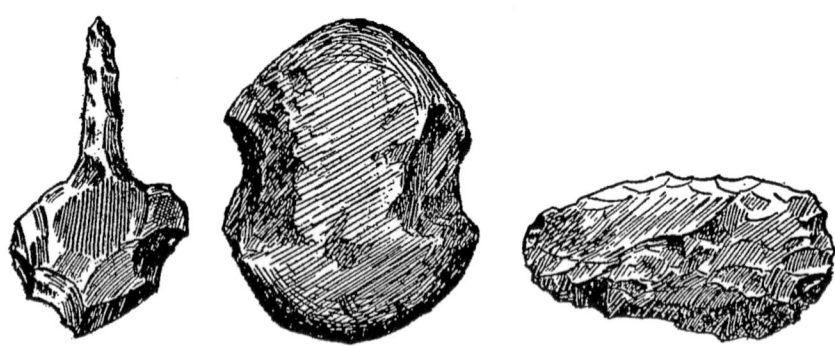

"BORER", NET-SINKER, AND "SCRAPER"

Of these three well-known types of implements, the "scraper" is the most common. Almost every village-site yields some of these handy utensils. The specimen here shown is a chipped fragment of milky-flint, and was found at "Moody's Rock", Sussex Co., N. J.

Another popular tool was the awl or "borer", used for perforating shells, bark, etc. This specimen is of jasper and was found at Trenton, N. J.

The net-sinker is found beside lakes and streams. That depicted above is a round field stone with "pecked" edges, and is from Hunterdon County, N. J. Quite often, very thin and flat stones were employed for this purpose.

squaw being limited, they "traveled light." Hence their household goods were limited to the barest necessaries. Luxury, to these primitive people, meant nothing more than a full stomach and a warm retreat. The struggle for existence and the capabilities of certain favored regions for providing sustenance were the controlling motives behind their frequent migrations. Of anything approaching "art" in their scheme of life, few traces are to be found apart from the perfection and occasional adornment of weapons and pottery, and the exceedingly rare "ceremonials" and trinkets for personal decoration—about which we shall endeavor to say something hereafter.

It is believed that the ability to make satisfactory pottery marks the highest point of development in the life of the American Indians prior to the coming of the Europeans. The squaw's heavy burden, when on the trail, consisted in large part of the dark-brown "crockery" which constituted a valued portion of her household furnishings. Fragments of these rough earthen vessels not only exist, but are very common on most Indian sites; nevertheless they are unrecognized, many times, by those who know and appreciate the value and significance of the flints.

One interesting fact concerning pottery should be set down. Almost invariably these fragments appear quite near the surface, seldom, if ever, being encountered at a greater depth than six inches. This means to the keenly observant scientist that they represent a period of culture existing towards the latter days of Indian tenancy in these parts. The earlier savages were, it seems, unacquainted with the potter's art. The specimens of this primitive earthenware which are found seem to date from the epoch immediately preceding the coming of the Europeans, and bear evidence to the fact that the Coastal Algonquin was beginning to develop a certain degree of perfection in this kind of handicraft. Some students are inclined to the belief that this knowledge had traveled overland from the red men of the Southwest, which is a plausible conjecture.

Perfect earthen vessels have rarely been found, for the reason, I suppose, that so long as they were serviceable it would have been folly to abandon them or impossible to lose them. The fragments we find are doubtless mementos of domestic accident, the result perhaps of some buxom squaw stumbling over a vessel placed carelessly or ill-advisedly; said vessel in consequence having met the fate which seems to be common to crockery in every day and age. One of the many mysteries which I have been unable to fathom is the invariable circumstance that while one frequently finds several small fragments which are undoubtedly parts of the same crock, and which in many instances fit together perfectly forming a larger fragment, he will seek in vain for the remaining pieces necessary to a restoration of the complete pot. His total findings of pot-sherds, while representing small pieces of many and varied utensils, will never yield "enough of a kind" to enable him to reconstruct more than one-eighth of a complete bowl. Whether or not such pottery was capable of being patched up and made water-tight, is a moot question. I think it must have been so, otherwise careful search would not fail to yield more nearly complete remains. Even new vessels, however, could not stand the long-continued stress of fire, hence the necessity of using "heat stones" which were taken from beneath the embers and thrown into the vessels when hot water was required for domestic purposes. It is well known, however, that broken pots were repaired and used for holding non-liquid substances; but in these cases, judging from perforated fragments which have been found, the pieces were laced together with thongs or withes.

I had not planned and do not intend to speak exhaustively upon the subject of pottery; but since I have waded inadvertently into deep water I must needs swim out. Fragments of so-called "decorated pottery" are common to all sites where there are other specimens of earthenware. The typical Algonquin designs are but adaptations of incised lines, often duplicated, varied by occasional rows of "pittings" possibly impressed upon the surface of the wet clay by means of a twig or a pipe stem. The rims of the utensils often show attempts at more elaborate border ornamentation, but always along the conventional lines. There are scant traces of portraiture of any kind. In a small shelter near Sloatsburg, N. Y., Mr. Max Schrabisch found four tiny representations of the human head, fashioned from clay, and apparently fragments of some unusually ornamented article of pottery. Dr. C. C. Abbott has given us record of a pipe-bowl similarly worked but these things are exceedingly rare in the East, and the amateur archaeologist cannot expect to find more than one such item in a lifetime, if at all.

Rarely, if ever, has an absolutely complete and perfect specimen of Indian pottery been discovered. Even those vessels found in aboriginal graves are invariably broken—perhaps this was done intentionally at the time of interment, for ceremonial reasons. I have seen single pieces recovered which were as large as the palm of my hand; and in some of the museums there are complete bowls reconstructed from fragments, and *almost* perfect. Should any of my readers be so fortunate as to find an *unbroken* vessel, I should advise its sale to one of the state museums. I am told that New Jersey is in the market for a perfect specimen, if found within the boundaries of the state, and thoroughly authenticated.

The acquaintance with Indian pottery and its appearance is a part of the business of the amateur archaeologist. It is easily distinguished from slate, shale, or even the brown glazed "bean-dish" ware of a century ago. Always rough and unglazed, it varies from 3/16 to 1/2 inch in thickness, and ranges in color from a yellow-buff to dark brown and black. No true red is ever encountered, so you need have no fear of confusing it with pieces of broken flower pots. Sometimes a specimen will reveal an admixture of shell-fragments—for the purpose, I infer, of toughening the vessel, although just how or why I fail to comprehend. Pottery is found to be either plain, "decorated," or "cord-marked," the last variety bearing the imprint of some unascertained fabric, possibly that of fishing nets, fashioned from rushes, and impressed upon the plastic surface of the unbaked vessel.

As to the method of making this primitive earthenware, I cannot imagine that the aborigines had any knowledge of the potter's wheel immortalized by the poet Omar and King David. I incline to the theory that certain artisans among the Indians were skilled in this particular work, as were others in fashioning artifacts of stone; but I think they employed the most primitive methods, possibly using round stones as moulds upon which to daub their prepared "mud" before the first sun-drying process; afterwards, maybe, filling them with sand for baking under a gentle heat. But I am open to conviction. Certainly the narrow-necked vessels required great skill in the making. Some anthropologists favor the theory that these vases were "built up" by coiling long ribbons of clay, but the fragments I have seen show not the slightest evidence that any such operation was employed.

STONE HATCHET
(with modern handle) showing one method of fastening to the stick. (See p. 49)

POTTERY FRAGMENT
decorated in the typical Algonquin manner. Portion of the rim of a vessel found near Franklin Lake, N. J.

CHAPTER IV.

BEFORE the coming of the white settlers, dense forests covered a large part of the Atlantic Seaboard States. When, therefore, we draw apart from the crowded city streets and plunge into the wildest stretches of remaining woodland, we are but transplanting ourselves to the natural environs of the red men. Within forty miles of Broadway there are expanses of rugged wilderness almost virgin in character; there are spots where sparkling cascades tumble over great bowlders beneath tall hemlocks and evergreens; there are dells whose seclusion seems never to have been disturbed since the hand of Nature drew the green curtain of privacy around them; there are rugged and wind-swept and glacier-scarred mountain tops from whose rocky pinnacles there may be seen a panorama of hill and valley extending from the Storm King on the Hudson to the blue line of sea and sky beyond Sandy Hook.

Doubtless the roving aborigines well knew these vantage points; mayhap their smoke signals were often broadcasted or their beacon fires kindled time and again upon the summits of the Ramapos or the Palisades where now, upon occasion, happy campers sit down to improvised luncheons beneath cloudless summer skies. The mountain tops, it is true, seldom reward the scientist with aboriginal mementos. On but one occasion have I heard of any "finds" in these lofty altitudes, and then but a solitary point. But the grand isolation of these "high places," the sense of kingship and dominion over the earth, and the feeling of companionship with the Creator, which come from mountain top experiences (whether upon the summit of the Biblical Horeb or the American Mount Beacon) justify an occasional drawing apart from the lowlands of endeavor to the heights of idealism. And, moreover, the upward climb out of civilization, through intervening valleys and over lesser heights, brings us truly in closest touch and contact with an untamed Nature —an acquaintance which goes hand-in-hand with an intimate knowledge of the simple children of Nature whom we, as a race, have dispossessed. Furthermore, woodland rambles often introduce us, most unexpectedly, to what I shall call the "occasional" habitations of the red-skins: those secondary sites, infrequently yet repeatedly used and occupied by Indian hunters while on the trail of game or when traveling from one more favored site to another.

It is a well-known fact that during the fall of the year or in the early spring, when the woods are more or less denuded of foliage, woodland exploration is greatly simplified. In luxuriant summer the wealth of verdure obscures the general characteristics of the mountains; rocks and caverns are less-easily seen; and oft-times the heat, even in the thick forest,

"BEAR ROCK" (Morris County, N. J.)

This granite boulder, of enormous size, was deposited during the glacial period. It lies five miles northeast of Boonton, about six miles west of Pompton Plains. Having been cloven in twain, it afforded two desirable shelters, each of which proved prolific in archaeological yield. A brook, which has never been known to dry up, flows down the valley within a few feet of the easterly shelter. Here thirty-two perfect arrowheads were unearthed, and upward of a thousand fragments and flakes. A perforated bear tooth, once part of a necklace, was without doubt the most interesting object found, well befitting the name by which the rock has been called for generations.

Structurally, it is just such a "rock of ages" as that in the cleft of which Chaplain Toplady having taken refuge from the storm, was inspired to write his now famous hymn.

"DARLINGTON ROCK HOUSE"
(*Bergen County, N. J.*)

Oftentime one is inclined to believe by reason of the multitude of well-identified Indian camp-sites and very evident tarrying-places scattered here and there amid the rugged wilderness—today infrequently visited save by hunters and ramblers—that the coastal Algonquin were a numerous people. It is authoritatively stated, however, that such was not the case. According to the highest estimates, New Jersey's prehistoric population never exceeded ten thousand, and some maintain that at times it dwindled to a thousand souls.

In making our calculations, therefore, we must perforce reckon upon a prolonged period of habitation as accounting for the abundance of remains. It should also be borne in mind that regions which seem to us as being exceedingly wild and remote, because they contrast so vividly with our congested and highly civilized communities, were but the accustomed and generally existing background of aboriginal life. The world of the American Indians was an environment of woods and rocks and trees—even their "centers of population" were but forest or river-side clearings. In the year of grace 1400, for example, "Darlington" was no more of an out-of-the-way wilderness than upper Manhattan, and no less favored. The strange Providence which has ordained that you and I should be born *who* we are, and *when* and *where,* has decreed enduring fame for some bits of mother earth and eternal obscurity for others.

is so oppressive as to make long-continued climbing quite laborious. Then again (especially if the region of the Ramapo Mountains be the field under survey) the rattle-snakes have to be reckoned with. It may be perfectly legitimate for Professor Ditmars of the Bronx Zoo to venture into these fastnesses with forked stick and persuasive words to lure combative *"crotalus"* from his sun-kissed rock; but I think the average archaeologist may safely yield these reptile conquests to a master of the art, and for himself remember that "discretion is the better part of valor." The black snake does no harm and had better be allowed to live in peace; likewise his humble cousins of the "garter" variety. "Rattlers" and "copper-heads," habitants respectively of the rocks and the swamps, are usually undesirous of an encounter with man; and if seen, it is the part of wisdom to give them a wide berth. When therefore the rambler finds himself enmeshed in mountainous country, especially in tempting huckleberry patches, the ear should be kept open for the cricket-like sound of Mr. Rattler's tail vibrations; and in the unavoidable descents into the tall grass of the marshes the nose should tilt with suspicion when the "cucumber" odor of the copper-head is scented. While man is the proverbial enemy of the snake (which to him is loathesome in the extreme), be it always remembered that the snake fears man in equal measure, and fights only in what seems to him to be self-defense. And snake-hunting is, at best, rather an ignoble pastime except for the scientist. You and I had better study botany or birds or Indians.

But as to times and seasons best suited for archaeological work. The fall of the year possesses a pathetic beauty, when full-ripened Nature regretfully awaits the chilling hand of winter. Spring, in like measure, seems all a-tingle with the prospect of eagerly awaited rejuvenation. To me, despite the sodden lowlands, heavy with melting snow, the early months of the year are the ideal time for woodland research. A bracing climb up and atop the heights; the descent

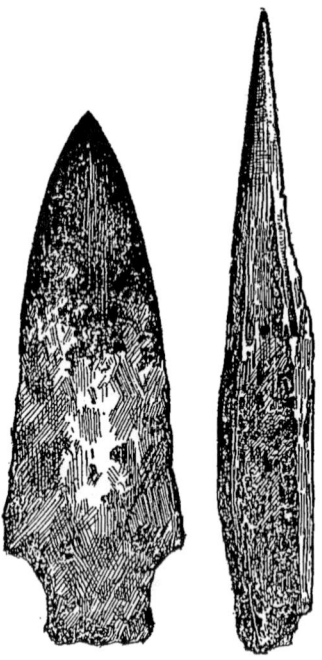

POLISHED POINT AND BONE AWL

Specimens showing a combination of the flaking and rubbing processes are of excessive rarity. Such an example, however, is furnished in the beautiful tip of purple argillite (herewith illustrated in exact size), the smoothed apex of which is sharpened like a dagger. It was picked up near the aboriginal argillite quarries at Flemington, N. J.

Equally interesting is the bone awl, found in "Panther Den", a popular Indian rendezvous beside the Beaver Kill, Sullivan County, N. Y. This type of aboriginal utensil, the point of which is polished to a nicety, served the purposes of "borer" and needle.

Both of these specimens are in the collection of Mr. Max Schrabisch of Paterson, N. J.

into the gullies—where, having escaped the penetrating rays of the sun, thick snow still lingers, fondly hiding in its embrace the trefoil leaves of the anemone—the welcome drink from clearest water in the madly rushing brooklets: these things tune up the body and the mind. Many a sheltering rock which has heretofore escaped notice, even in supposedly well-examined localities, yields its treasures to the springtime adventurer; and the access to many a hillside cavern, usually blocked by a tangle of laurel or brambles, is rendered surprisingly easy to the venturesome explorer who "rushes the season" in his romantic quest.

I shall presently refer to noteworthy rock-shelters and cliffs. May I now speak of three very "ordinary" sites (when the matter of results is reckoned) but very enchanting from the standpoint of environment and incidental contact with ambient Nature. These going and coming experiences, and the "types" of proven haunts of ancient dwellers in the woodland wilderness, may serve to guide my friends in other sections of the country to similar forgotten nooks and corners of their own home neighborhood.

Dear old Dr. Russell Conwell, in his lecture, "Acres of Diamonds," tells of the searcher who vainly traveled the world in his quest for riches, only to find the hidden store beneath his own vine and fig tree. The allegory seems often to apply to aboriginal research. I know a certain "back yard" in the heart of the city of Paterson which I have reason to think would, if carefully excavated, yield many curious traces of the red men. (But I am saving the pleasure for myself when conditions are favorable.) "Where ignorance is bliss, 'tis folly to be wise"—this much for the present occupant of the premises, who has an unappreciative soul.

My first humble site, typical of countless others all over the land, I have always referred to as the "Darlington rock," because it is contiguous to a neighborhood bearing that pretty name, near the Ramapo River in the upper corner of New Jersey's county of Bergen. For those of my readers who may by chance reside in New Jersey, let me say that it is near the so-called Bear Swamp. The accompanying illustration will serve to show that the "shelter" is afforded by a conspicuous outcropping of the gneissic rock which underlies the entire region round about. Like every other similar protuberance in the neighborhood, the stratifications seem to open up with a western exposure—in itself an auspicious sign—for such spots, favored by the afternoon sun, must have seemed to the prowling savage mightily attractive in chilly autumn days. Beneath the "overhang" in the middle distance, upon a rock-bedded floor surface which offered little prospect, we made three finds: a broken spear-head of quartz, quite ungainly (as is usually the case with this material); an almost perfect triangular bird-point of black flint; and a tiny fragment of a clay pipestem—most likely a relic of trading intercourse with the early Dutch settlers. Not much, indeed, but amply sufficient for the purpose of telling us the story that this crude natural refuge had been deemed worthy of visitation. It has always been my conjecture that the red-skins temporarily improved such spots by making a sort of "lean-to" of saplings, sloping outward, which they contrived to cover with skins or blankets, thereby making a half-tepee under which a fire, with a suitable smoke outlet, gave its full benefit to the transients who here sought refuge from the elements between the going down of the sun and its next rising.

There are sections of northern New Jersey where the mountains are so littered with great bowlders that one almost believes that these hills, instead of being natural elevations of the earth's crust, are rather gigantic piles of individual rocks. Clambering up slopes such as these is like making the ascent of the great pyramid of Cheops, save that these giant steps are of gneiss, hard as adamant, covered with lichens and beautified by moss; whereas the monuments beside the Nile are fashioned from piled-up blocks of fossiliferous limestone. But as regards the ups and downs of the matter, the similarity is striking. And the Indian site about which I now propose to expatiate is one, found by merest chance, among such a shaded tangle of rocks and fallen trees and wild laurel, on one of the "topsy-

THE ROCK-GIRT COVERT AT LAKE MACOPIN
(See pages 64-67-68 of text)

The "Homes and Haunts of the Indians" are and always will be a part of our heritage as their successors to the proud title of "Americans"—and particularly as citizens of the United States. And, lest it should be thought that our adopted regional ancestry be that of a people devoid of those inherent qualities by which present-day character is measured, may the writer be permitted to digress from the realm of the essay to that of history, if for no other purpose than to pay tribute to one *good* Indian. Had not the influence of the whites been so entirely foreign and over-powering, there might have been many other shining examples—to share with us our vaunted "culture" and present-day civilization.

From out the dim past, when settler and Indian had a contact all too brief, comes the name of venerable Oratam,* sachem of the Achkinkeshacky (Hackensack) tribe of the Lenni Lenape, whose long life spanned the years 1577-1667, who saw the coming of the Dutch and English and, realizing the inevitable, strove to play the man, the peace-maker and the good citizen under the new order of things. In the early records of the proceedings between the Dutch Government at New Amsterdam and the Indians of the lower Hudson and neighboring regions, we find Oratam throwing himself and his weighty influence into the breach when the more war-like Raritans or Wappings or Nyacks or Esopus Indians meditated justifiable but vain attempts against the conquerors who had come to stay.

* See "The Indians of Bergen County" (N. J.), Frances A. Westervelt, 1923.

GARRET MOUNTAIN ROCK-SHELTER
(Paterson, N.J.)

Against the towering cliff which forms the eastern face of Paterson's great stone mountain leans a gigantic fragment of the basaltic mother-rock, pushed from its original anchorage atop the height by glacial pressure. That the admirable natural shelter thus afforded—which, with a little elaboration, could have been made impervious to the elements—was availed of many times by the Indians, has been abundantly proven. So hidden must it have been in ancient times that marauding war-parties could have passed along the valley trail not far distant without suspecting its existence. While the Lenape Indians of these parts were a peaceful people, to the best of our knowledge, there were doubtless occasions when visitors in large numbers, less amicably disposed, moved through their territory. Under such circumstances we may suppose that the local natives, unless numerous enough to command the respect of the strangers or give them battle, kept themselves carefully hidden. Such a nook as this secluded "lean-to" would have been an ideal covert for a small party of observers.

turvy" hillsides bordering beautiful Lake Macopin, some five miles from Newfoundland, in the county of Morris. Known formerly as Echo Lake, it used to be a favored resort for excursionists and picnic parties; but now, since it has become one of the sources of a municipal supply of potable water, it is "restricted." It is a so-called "natural lake," and, as such, its shore lines present much the same contour as in Indian times. According to the accounts of the farmers dwelling in the region to the south, many relics have been found along its banks.

To the north of this silvery pond is a patch of swampy ground, flanked by the thickly wooded base of Kanouse Mountain. Along this slope the massive bowlders of which I have spoken are tumbled about in greater confusion than usual. Snakes abound; indeed, for utter wilderness and loneliness, I think this region ranks second to none.

Yet, amidst all these obstructions, we found a hitherto unsuspected rock-dwelling. While prowling around near the water, our attention was attracted to a dark hollow a little way up the hillside. Laboriously we clambered over the treacherous rocks, making sure of our footing before each step, and soon found ourselves facing a small cavern formed by Nature in one of her sportive moods. After a few moments spent in "cleaning house" of the accumulated loam and vegetation of a century and a half, we came upon the "Indian level." There, before our eyes, were innumerable fragments of pottery, which had lain thus undisturbed for all these years! Still more came to light after a little work with the trowel; then the usual bones, and an abundance of the shells of fresh water mussels, showing that the primitive occupants of the cave had been fond of the dainties afforded by the nearby lake. Then, at a corner of the rock, other pieces of earthenware were found from which the rains of many years had washed all traces of earth. Indeed these specimens were entirely exposed.

FRAGMENT OF DECORATED IROQUOIAN POTTERY

This unusual specimen, a portion of the rim of a large earthen vessel, shows a representation of what appears to be the human face.

It was found by Mr. Max Schrabisch near Cuddebackville, beneath a limestone rock-shelter contiguous to the Basha Kill upon the western slope of the Shawangunk Mountains.

Most of the pottery proved to be quite dark, almost black; and was of the variety which experts call "cord-marked." The outer surfaces of the fragments gave us the impression that the vessels, before they were hardened, had been patted with some woven fabric, possibly Indian nets made from grasses or rushes. Chips were not at all numerous beneath this lowly shelter, and but one perfect specimen was found: a beautiful little triangular arrow point of black flint.

The Lake Macopin rock-house is an illustration of Nature fashioning a habitation by dropping great blocks of stone one upon another; the Darlington site represented the utilization by the Indians of an ungainly mal-formation upon the back of mother earth. There is yet another type of rock-shelter, fairly common hereabout, which was likewise improved by the wandering children of the forest, who seem to have known every nook and corner of the woodland. I refer to instances where large bowlders lean one against another, tent fashion; or where a lesser monolith lies aslant against some frowning ledge of extrusive basaltic traprock. Two such sites come to my mind: the one adjacent to the Great Piece Meadows of Morris County, not far from Towaco, on the line of the D. L. & W. R. R.; the other just outside the limits of the City of Paterson, beneath the shadow of Garret Mountain, which is compassed within the estate of the late Catholina Lambert, art collector and silk manufacturer. A photograph of the latter is more serviceable than descriptive words, and is given as purely a matter of instruction, as my own intimacy with the site concerns many mountain rambles rather than scientific research, for it affords an attractive retreat and is a wonderful place in which to build a camp fire and cook supper on a wintery day after an afternoon's tramp over the mountain. Mr. Schrabisch, who thoroughly explored this site, has thus described it:

> "The excavation of the shelter close to the cliff brought to light flint chips, scrapers, several broken arrow points, and pottery fragments, as well as deer and muskrat bones. The one drawback to this otherwise splendid rockhouse was the absence of water in the immediate vicinity. This explains why the investigation did not result in more and better finds, and merely establishes the fact that some red-skins had occasionally camped under this rock, building a fire and chipping a few artifacts."

We who live in Paterson are proud of Garret Mountain, which rises high above our great commercial city like some giant sentinel. It is to us what "Mars Hill" was to ancient Athens. Yet, archaeologically, it is by no means rich. Besides the shelter above described, there is a bowlder and a cave, each of which has yielded a few primitive implements, and atop the imposing "Acropolis" there are some four or five scattered camp sites. To a visiting stranger, however, it would seem that our mountain must surely abound in every form of Indian treasure. The answer to the implied query is just this, that the aborigines were creatures of expediency. They would not cross a rugged mountain when a river-bank trail served their purpose equally well; they much preferred a sunny valley to a wind-swept height; they struggled manfully to exist; and to win enduring fame by leaving monuments upon the mountain-tops was the farthest of all thoughts from their simple minds.

"CEDAR POND ROCK"
The massive monolith some five miles west of Stony Point, Rockland Co.,N. Y., where the author was initiated into the mysteries of Indian Rock Shelters.

CHAPTER V.

A GIANT glacial bowlder amid the deep solitudes of the forest, with a natural pond not far away and a merry brooklet vainly endeavoring to rouse us from the lethargy of a mid-summer day—this was the scenic background which witnessed my initiation into the mysteries of Indian rock-shelters. My friend, Mr. Schrabisch, is justly entitled to the honor of having been the first to call public attention to the fact that sheltering ledges of rock were a favorite habitat of the red men in the region contiguous to New York City. European scientists had long been aware of similar circumstances in the old world; American savants acquiesced; but it remained for Mr. Schrabisch to penetrate the bowlder-strewn and hilly country of northern New Jersey and southern New York and bring forth from out the blackened soil beneath the sheltering cliffs many surprising traces of the ancient people who had loved and frequented these points of vantage.

The subject of aboriginal dwellings or transient abodes beneath the rocks is, I suppose, a matter chiefly of interest to those who dwell in a similarly favored region. Without information to the contrary, I shall presume that every ledge of rock which might suffice to shelter a wandering hunter or trapper of the present day—overtaken by storm or nightfall—has been used for the same purpose time and again by prehistoric man, and therefore the soil beneath it may hold much in the way of hidden secrets of the past, which await the diligent search of the excavator. Rock shelters, when discovered, almost instantly reveal to the student an absence or lack of certain prerequisites. If the "over-hang" is meagre, if there be an absence of good water near at hand, or if the sheltered area be a water-washed bit of mother-rock, you may as well save your energies. But if the reverse conditions are at once apparent, and if, beneath the accumulated layer of long-dead leaves, you find a hard-packed earthen floor—thank kind Providence, draw forth your inquisitive trowel, and bend your back to the task. The most favorable "first indication" is a level of charcoal-blackened earth. If this be found you may look for the remains of ancient fires, with bits of charred bone and pot-sherds, interspersed with occasional chips of flint. Such a "culture level" is the richest possible field for worth-while finds, and you may confidently expect some more or less perfect artifacts, with the ever-present possibility of bringing to light choice specimens of primitive handiwork which may have been lost or secreted in a much-frequented haunt of long-forgotten days. Such a rendezvous was my first Indian Rock, now denominated as "Cedar Pond Rock Shelter," and lying some five miles to the west of Stony Point-on-Hudson.

Mr. Schrabisch, in his wanderings, had somehow or other become apprised of the existence of this rock, which local tradition had invested with a number of romantic stories, among which was one to the effect that long ago a recluse had built about its sheltering sides a wooden "lean-to," and here had lived for many years. The rock itself is really noteworthy, its equal in size being rarely encountered even in a region liberally sprinkled with glacial erratics. Pentagonal in shape, its total circumference is nearly one hundred feet, its height averaging thirty-five to forty. Three of its five "facets" offer comfortable overhanging roofs and beneath them, upon first sight, Mr. Schrabisch saw traces of Indian tenancy long antedating the proprietorship of the lone white man. He had already devoted a week to this site before my visit, having found it an exceedingly prolific field of labor. When therefore in response to his note of invitation I journeyed to Stony Point, I found that he had already done much in the way of preliminary work and had brought to light an exceedingly interesting assortment of curios. Besides this he had made the acquaintance of every farmer in the neighborhood and cultivated a still stronger bond of friendship for one of the canine members of the household where he was billeted. As a matter of course, the dog made himself one of the party on this particular day of days, knowing full well that compensation would be his in the way of an unusually ample luncheon. One of my "first impressions" on this, my maiden expedition to the haunts of the Indians, was the comment of the master-archaeologist that, as a rule, country dogs are under-fed, accompanied by the admonition always to bring a supply of eatables sufficient to provide a bun or two for such four-footed friends as we might encounter en route. Subsequent "chance acquaintances" with farmers' dogs have proven this to be true. The back-woods tramper will be abundantly rewarded for his generosity if he, likewise, will be liberal with the gaunt but amiable mongrels who form so faithful and yet so unappreciated a portion of our rural population.

As we plodded along the highway from the shores of the majestic Hudson to our goal in the wooded fastnesses of the "hinterland"—(our road being the undoubted successor to an aboriginal trail, since it followed and wormed around the hills in conformity with the creek)—my instructive mentor outlined some of the first principles of Indian "trailing," emphasizing the fact that we should never lose the picture of the woods and valleys, brooks and rivers, cliffs and meadows, *as they were* before the "improvements" of the settlers, if we expect to locate with precision the homes and haunts of the erstwhile denizens of the forest. It is astonishing how insignificant "miles" become when one is in the delectable company of congenial or well-informed friends. To tramp alone may have its enjoyments, but for myself I feel inclined to pity the solitary traveler. Surely if he cannot find someone who knows *more* than himself, he can "scare up" a companion whom he can, in turn, benefit and instruct. The beauties of the woodland and the delights of travel, give an hundred-fold of enjoyment to those who share them with others. After having on two occasions toured Europe and the Orient unaccompanied (save for the chance companionship of strangers equally lonesome), I have become convinced that pleasures shared are pleasures doubled. And so,

DETAIL OF "CEDAR POND ROCK"
(*Showing ancient smoke-stains, reminiscent of Indian fires*)

"Some minds are irresistibly drawn to a contemplation of the past. To unravel the mysteries of bygone ages, to lift the veil which separates the known from the unknown, is to them an occupation productive of the purest joys. Enthralled by that fascination for the subject which seems to overcome all difficulties, no expenditure of time and labor is deemed too great so long as by such efforts some tangible results may be obtained. And, to be sure, archaeology or the science of antiquities has many charms. It offers to its disciples a field as vast as the habitable part of the globe, and one which—as regards the United States of America—is as yet but little explored. To visit and investigate the former camping-grounds, village-sites and habitations of aboriginal peoples is to him who loves this occupation, a source of real gratification. It is here that he gathers the material which furnishes the sole foundation for his science. It is here that he wistfully harks back, trying to wrest the mystery from the inexorable past, which, deaf to his entreaties, leaves him to his own ingenuity."

—Max Schrabisch.

"GOLF HILL" ROCK HOUSE
(Orange County, N. Y.)

In the text I have spoken in detail as to the "findings" beneath this attractive overhang. The scientific method of excavating such a promising site is far different from mere surface scratching. Usually one or more trenches are dug across the sheltered area, the thrown-up earth being carefully screened and sifted for tell-tale clues. Such a method often reveals an interesting cross section of varied stratum; demonstrating sometimes that between a period of very ancient occupancy and much later visitations there was an unexplainable lapse of many years.

Mr. M. R. Harrington, who has done much work of this character in Westchester County, N. Y., found at "Finch's Rock House" on Mianus River indisputable evidence of two distinct periods of aboriginal tenancy. Between the near-surface layer of relic-bearing soil and a bed-rock accumulation of equally prolific character, appeared, as he puts it, "yellow sand, which had sifted in and washed down over the deserted hearths. . . . How long a period this represents, when the rock-house stood untenanted, no man can say, but when the Indians came back they had pottery—well-made decorated pottery. Then life began again, much as before: the deer was still hunted, shellfish still brought from distant places, refuse accumulated. . . . These latter people saw the first coming of the white man. They accepted his wonderful gifts, his guns, his unbreakable shining arrow points of brass, his beautiful white clay pipes—all very useful in their way. . . . Then came the final gifts of civilization to the Indian: whiskey, smallpox and death. So the book was closed, the story written, and the fox and the woodchuck again took possession."

the way to Cedar Pond Rock was not *five miles* at all, it was two hours of expectancy and exhilaration.

When at last we detoured from the much-traveled highway and entered the forest by a well-nigh overgrown wagon road, I was prepared for anything, even a face-to-face meeting with some of the astonished savages who must upon this very ground have discussed in great agitation and wonderment the strange and unique sight of Hudson's white-winged argosy as it passed up the North River bound for the unknown.

Cedar Pond Rock well justified my expectations, as it will those of my readers who may essay to seek and find it, save that it has been robbed of all but its scenic treasures. Now, after a dozen years, I doubt not that a new blanket of damp and withered leaves has covered the scars of spade and trowel; and to the casual observer I believe no traces of disturbance would be apparent. Such are the processes of Nature, the healer and the beautifier.

At the Cedar Pond Rock, as in the case of many another similar site, hundreds of troublesome stones, large and small, had to be removed from around its base before satisfactory results were possible of attainment. Beneath the most favorable of its sheltering sides a full four-foot accumulation of rocks lay between the eager researcher and the bona fide ground-level. But when, by dint of much physical labor (performed during the early morning hours) the base of the monolith was exposed to view, it proved to be blackened by the smoke stains of numberless aboriginal camp-fires ! Thus, I found it, when introduced to its colossal bulk. Since then, the thrill of these unmistakable signs of long-smothered fires has somewhat waned, through familiarity; but I well recollect that, at the time, I was profoundly impressed. Of course, the earth beneath the sooty wall was equally discolored

—in fact, for an average depth of two feet and more there was little else but a co-mingling of charcoal and loam, liberally interspersed as I soon found, with bits of charred deer and bear bones, attesting to many wholesome feasts. I still possess a box full of this so-called "Indian junk" which I carried home as being equal in value to so much gold. Of course this rubbish is thrown into the discard by those who know the game, as are the multitude of flint and argillite "chips" which are encountered in excavating a shelter such as this. They mean little, it is true, in a place so rich in remains as was Cedar Pond Rock; but I have known instances where one or two of these little "slivers" of fractured stone, found in a locality otherwise barren, have established the fact beyond dispute that some wandering red-skin passed that way. But at Cedar Pond, if every chip had a story to tell, we should be listening yet, for here they appeared by the peck—large and small, of every conceivable shape, varying in material from the basest of slate to exquisite yellow jasper and iolite.

I don't think I ever knew the exact toll of perfect specimens which were yielded by this rock-house. At the time of my visit the work was but half-completed, and before quitting the locality Mr. Schrabisch became the richer by upward of two hundred arrow and spear-heads, some fragments of pottery of unusually generous size, many hand-hammers and pestles, and—if I remember correctly—a fair specimen of a stone hatchet and some broken ceremonial stones.* As we worked together on the day of my visit, I saw many of these things come forth out of the ground, myself finding only some small pieces of pottery. But, as this was my first experience, you may be sure that I eagerly confiscated all the outcast bones and chips.

* All of these specimens are now at the American Museum of Natural History, New York City.

I learned much, however, which I have never forgotten; and the unexplored "rock-shelter" will always be, for me, a site of great possibility.

Quite another type of sheltering rock is that herewith illustrated as "Golf Hill," and from beneath the friendly overhang of this protruding mountain side I was permitted to gather my first actual harvest of flints. Fourteen fine points constituted my share of the booty on the delightful day during which we labored here. The rock faces the west, receiving the benefit of every afternoon of sunshine, and it must have been a very comfortable retreat for the shivering savages, who, 'mid winter's rigors, had plodded over the wind-swept trail which was their accustomed highway from the Minisink Country to the South. The modern "back road" from Monroe to Southfields (both places in Orange County, N. Y.) passes within sight of the formidable ledge, being separated from it by a narrow stretch of low-lying meadow land, probably once a swamp offering ideal covert for the wild turkey and other "game birds" which were so abundant hereabout in prehistoric times.

Structurally, the shelter was exceedingly well adapted to such elaborations as any band of red-skins who decided to winter here might choose to make. The rocky roof permitted a standing-room area of at least three hundred square feet, with many nooks and niches at the base of the towering precipice where a tired brave might squat and smoke his pipe in peace and contentment. As is usual in the case of rock-shelters, certain spots, when thoroughly examined with the trowel, appeared to have been ancient fire-places, and around them the pottery and flints and bones were distributed most liberally. Among other things, we found many traces of occupancy by white men: fragments of old blue china, broken bottles, and bits of iron such as harness buckles, rings and part of a bit. In the face of the cliff there was moreover an imbedded iron ring. Some of the country people told us, as we trudged back to Southfields, that long ago a farmhouse stood beside the road near Golf Hill, and that a barn had been built against the cliff. This probably explains the presence of the iron ring in the rock, and also shows that the white man resorted to the same expedients as did the Indians who preceded him, by erecting a stockade around a natural overhang of rock and availing of its shelter.

Southfields, Tuxedo, Sloatsburg, and Ramapo, stations of the Erie Railroad's trunk line, are but milestones upon one of the most picturesque and well-traveled aboriginal trails in the East. Through a beautiful defile of the Ramapo mountains fifteen miles in length runs a silvery rivulet, and beside it a state highway and the railroad. The records of the Revolutionary period refer to this gap in the hills as "Smith's Clove," or the "Ramapo Clove," and the steep and heavily wooded hills which flank the ancient road have witnessed the passing of every notable character who played a part in the struggle for independence. An entire volume might be devoted to the "Homes and Haunts of the Indians along the Ramapo," so numerous are the traces of their lingerings beside this favored stream. First and foremost, I think, among the landmarks of the narrow valley, is that striking monolith which keeps watch and ward over the defile at Tuxedo, just a quarter-mile to the north of the entrance to the Park. "Man-of-war Rock" it has been called, because its peculiar shape suggests the towering prow of a battleship. Tradition has it that, in the days when the Orange County militia strove to defend the pass against roving and predatory bands of the enemy, some of the patriots took stand behind this natural bar-

"MAN-OF-WAR ROCK"
(Near the entrance to Tuxedo Park, Orange Co., N. Y.)

This prehistoric rock-shelter had many advantageous features to commend it; and its consequent popularity—evidenced by the numerous traces of Indian tenancy strewn about its base—is a source of but little surprise. Before it passed a highly favored trail—the logical avenue of north and south communication—and, but a few yards distant, ran the sprightly Ramapo River.

The nomadic proclivities of the savage led him often to seek new hunting grounds, and in his migrations he undoubtedly availed of certain favored bivouacs. There can be no doubt that Man-of-War Rock, with its crude hospitalities, was a well-remembered caravansary to such red-skins as frequently traversed this wind-swept defile. In 1718, the Tuscarora Indians, coming up from the South, passed northward through the Ramapo Valley on their way to join the Five Nations. At Suffern, near the New Jersey line, where the hills melt away into a more gentle type of landscape, several Indian trails diverged. One continued along the Ramapo to Oakland and Pompton, another wended its way southward toward Hohokus, a third made for the Hudson near Haverstraw. In each instance modern highways follow these ancient trails beaten by the moccasined feet of the forgotten pathfinders.

BENEATH THE SHELTER OF "HORSE STABLE ROCK"
(Ramapo Mountains, near Tuxedo, N. Y.)

"To him whose mind is of an archaeological turn the exploration of an aboriginal rock-shelter is an undertaking of the most fascinating kind. To such a one these places are invested with an irresistible charm, for it is here, in the well-defined space underneath the rock, that he fancies to come nearer to the red-man—to enter into greater intimacy with him.

"In contrast with field work, which necessitates the search of ancient village-sites, of ploughed fields along the banks of lakes, rivers and brooks, he here finds everything localized in one spot, narrow and circumscribed, with the element of guess-work entirely eliminated. Often he wishes that the rocks might be privileged to speak, so that they could tell of the long ago happenings beneath their hospitable roofs. But, alas, all he can do is draw his own conclusions, more or less correct, from the evidence extant—aided in his conjectures by the insight born of long experience."

—Max Schrabisch.

ricade on one occasion, and succeeded in "picking off" several among the ranks of the invaders, thereby turning the purposes of their expedition.

Archaeologically, it is a site of great promise and fecundity, although despoiled in a measure by repeated visits of those knowing its secrets. Similar, in many respects, to the great bowlder near Cedar Pond, its southern and western shelters yielded the most noteworthy curios. I shall not go into a detailed account of what has here been found, but I mention the site as being the most easily reached of any of the first-class rock-shelters of which I have knowledge. It is but a dozen feet from the state road, and you may stop your motor car for a moment or two whenever you pass that way to give it a hurried inspection. Without doubt there is much "treasure" yet to be found here by anyone who will systematically circle the giant rock, and thoroughly sift the soil 'round about. And I doubt not that a very superficial survey will reveal to sharp eyes some of the rejected chips thrown out by those of the confraternity of amateurs who have here labored awhile and then become "weary in well-doing."

But the Indian crag which, above all others in these parts, has been to me a never-failing source of delight, is the so-called "Horse-stable Rock" situated upon the mountains in the most inaccessible part of the Ramapos, and crowning one of the highest vantage points of the range. It so happens that "Man-of-war Rock," of which I have spoken, gives the clue to its whereabouts, for just across the Ramapo River an eastward and constantly ascending wood-cutters' road, gradually diminishing to a scarcely recognizable trail, leads from the noisy haunts of men to the vast silences of the top of the world.

I have visited Horse-stable Rock on four or five

occasions. Mr. Schrabisch once told me he had been there upwards of fifty times, and I know of many other visitors who, likewise, delight in repeating the experience. As may be imagined the site has been pretty nearly robbed of all its Indian treasures in consequence of its popularity. If, therefore, you set out to find it, expect rather to enjoy Nature in her wildest beauty than to return with bulging pockets, full of clinking flints.

The inaccessibility of Horse-stable Rock was the feature which prompted Claudius Smith, a royalist of the Revolutionary period who preyed upon the patriot farmers of the Ramapo valley, to select it as his safe and secure retreat when threatened with pursuit and capture. His supposed practice of stabling stolen horses in this mountain covert while awaiting a favorable opportunity to get them within the British lines and reap the reward of his knavery, has given the place its peculiar name. You will find the story of Claudius, "The Cowboy of the Ramapo Valley," in an interesting volume, half fiction, half fact, written by P. Demarest Johnson some thirty years ago—now, unfortunately, out of print, but of which I have a copy.

As the crow flies, Horse-stable Rock is but two and a half miles east of Tuxedo, but it is one of the most difficult places to locate, especially as changing seasons alter the aspect of the intervening ridges; and a winter identification would be of little service in the case of a summer-time revisitation. Even those familiar with these mountains sometimes go astray, as there are several rocky ledges of similar appearance, these terraces being broken up and complicated by little cross-valleys and gullies, swampy patches and jungle interspersing heaps of gigantic bowlders—all at an altitude approximating a thousand feet above tide water. The visitor should, moreover, beware of several dangerous mine holes, relics of long-abandoned quests for iron, which add to the natural obstacles of the wilderness.

In many respects, Horse-stable Rock is the monarch of aboriginal rock shelters. Those of my readers who live in regions far removed from the Atlantic Coast may find its counterpart; but hereabouts it has no rival in point of structure and yield of relics. Mr. Schrabisch, the discoverer of its archaeological significance, admits that his first efforts in this direction were not prompted by ethnological interest, but rather to verify the vague rumors concerning its Revolutionary history. In this perfectly legitimate quest he was rewarded, and local tradition was confirmed in large measure, by the discovery of three large English copper coins of 1729 and 1739, and four mold-cast leaden bullets, seeming to lend color to the story that armed men had resorted, on occasion, to this out-of-the-way place.

The rock itself faces the west, overlooking a comparatively level tract of upland swamp, covered with luxuriant vegetation. There is a sheltered area of some seventy feet in length, and in places the roof protrudes full fifteen feet, being for the most part quite lofty. This protected lair, the floor of which even the snows of mid-winter fail to cover, constitutes the main "apartment" of the fabled bandit rendezvous, while some eighty feet higher up, on the very top of the cliff, there is a transverse crevice in the rocks which would offer make-shift shelter, and which is reputed to have been the "look-out" of the infamous guerilla band. Today you, too, may clamber to the summit, and view a panorama which, for expanse and beauty, is unrivaled this side of the Catskills. The experience is a positive revelation to anyone who labors under the delusion that it is necessary to visit the White Mountains, or Switzerland, or our great Northwest, in order to touch the fringes of the firmament.

But, descending again to the level of the more significant portion of the retreat—so far as the traces of man are concerned—let us recall a few noteworthy facts. Near the extreme left, water trickles through a fissure on the inner wall, collecting in a natural basin which is always filled, excepting during periods of great drought; and at the head of the swamp to the north of the rock there is a spring of excellent water, which never fails. This fact alone would have been a feature commending the spot alike to roving Indian and skulking horse-thief. That the former was partial to this mountain retreat, long before the intrusion of white men or horses, is amply proven by the fact that Mr. Schrabisch collected from the spot nearly two hundred specimens of primitive handiwork, embracing spear and arrow points of all the shapes, sizes and materials known in these parts, besides thousands of flakes and bones—some of the latter still lying about the premises. The bones represented members of the deer family, besides the bear, wolf, raccoon, opossum, and beaver. There were found two deer's horns, and a beaver tooth, the latter gracefully curved and four inches long. Not a vestige of pottery came to light, this absence of earthenware being accounted for, doubtless, by the fact that the rock was quite remote from the nearest aboriginal settlement, and to carry pottery over miles of exceedingly rough country such as this would have been cumbersome and useless.

I do not know whether I have so described Horse-stable Rock as to permit the formation of an adequate mental picture, or to indicate the wide variety of interesting things which may be found in a similarly favored spot; but I sincerely hope that some equally important place of prehistoric significance will suddenly confront you on one of your wilderness jaunts.

Never do the Ramapo Mountains display greater charms for the lover of Nature than in mid-winter; and no more delightful time for a visit to Horse-stable Rock can be imagined. The foaming Ramapo River beneath the swinging bridge at Tuxedo is now ice-fringed. The little settlement through which you pass, with its tiny log cottages and roofs heavily snow-laden, suggests an Alpine village. White and well-trodden woodland paths gradually give place to trails through deep snow. The suggestive tracks of the wild things of the forest begin to cross and re-cross the snow-shoe prints of someone who has obligingly broken the trail before us at the first familiar detour. We plod upward into the fragrant "pine belt." The grove which seemed so dark and sombre last summer has been transformed, as if by the magic wand of Nature, into a Christmas fairyland. Towering hemlock, dwarf cedar, and cone-laden pine, all have become greener and more beautiful by contrast with their now leafless neighbors, and by the diffused radiance of myriad snow crystals which weigh heavily upon their bending boughs and cover the ground beneath with a Yuletide blanket. Nor can the mountain laurel or the red-berried wintergreen be suppressed; and even the supposedly delicate fern is in evidence here and there. They peep above the snow, these old friends, and bid us hearty welcome.

The waterfall where we were wont to pause during the fatiguing climb of many a glorious June, has yielded to the spell of winter and fallen asleep. Frozen into a curtain of lace, it now drapes the cascade stairway to the mountain top. Here again we halt, as of yore, and, in the tarrying, are permitted to behold the dream of the sleeping cataract. Behind the ice, a tiny aperture offers admittance to a miniature sanctuary, separated from the world without by a rood-screen of diamonds the like of which no cathedral in the universe could boast, and illumined by a mellow and almost holy light.

And so it is all along the upward trail. The prints of the snow-shoes have vanished: whoever wore them having doubtless been seduced into the tracking of some predatory fox. And we clamber to the heights through undisturbed and loosely drifting snow, from rock to rock, and over fallen tree-trunks, until at last we see the patriarch of the mountains in his winter garb, and—sheltered from the blast—kindle the great fire for the evening feast.

Do you know from experience the joys of the out-door world? The solace of congenial companionship around the blazing bivouac logs? The peaceful sleep of the tired tramper, and the glories of a new day born amid the mountains? These pleasures may be essentially primitive, but they make or re-make a man.

And to him who wakes beneath the shadow of an Indian rock, and contemplates the deep sapphire sky of the West, studded with its faintly twinkling stars, fading reluctant before approaching dawn—will come an undying admiration and understanding love for the aboriginal American people who have likewise passed into the land of memory.

THE INDIAN KEPT IN REMEMBRANCE
(*Montclair, Essex Co., N. J.*)

Before the Museum of Fine Arts in this beautiful suburban town, the picturesque bronze by H. A. MacNeil (Rome, 1902), sometimes interpreted as "the Sun Vow," keeps alive the recollection of the primitive people who once-upon-a-time frequented these lovely heights. Within the museum—a most praise-worthy institution for a residential community—there is a notable collection of Indian curios, many of which were found in the immediate neighborhood.

Not more than a mile distant is celebrated "Eagle Rock," vantage point of the aborigines, and county reservation of the present day. From its lofty height a view may be obtained of New York City and the populous "Metropolitan area" extending well into New Jersey, in which it is said fully one-tenth of the population of the United States reside.

MacNeil's group appeals to everyone because of the boy with up-turned face. May it be true of each of the splendid lads of today who, on occasion, wander in to the "Indian room" or gaze but half-comprehending at the paintings and curios, that kindly and maturer minds may lead them along the ever-ascending trail—that they too may learn to face the sun. They are the Americans of the future; in their keeping lies the destiny of our Republic.

THE SITE OF OLD "JAMES TOWNE"

(Showing the recently-erected monuments to Captain John Smith and Pocahontas)

No locality in America possesses such interest for the historian and the student of Indian lore as does this island on the James River, separated from the mainland by a marsh-bordered creek, where from 1607 to 1698 stood James Towne, "the first American Metropolis".

Today it is a deserted village: there being no remains of the ancient town which was once the capital of Virginia save the ivy-mantled church-tower and its adjoining grave-yard. Nevertheless, the visitor realizes that he stands upon a spot whereon were determined the destinies of the New World, for here English colonists established their first permanent foot-hold, despite the adverse circumstances of famine and pestilence, combined with a natural hostility on the part of the aboriginal inhabitants. There, moreover, our first governmental and communal experiments were put into practice. Without question, it was a place much frequented by the Indians for years beyond number before the coming of the white settlers.

Recently, an imposing sea-wall has been erected to protect the hallowed spot from the encroachments of the James estuary, a modern chapel has been added to the venerated tower and a beautiful "Anglo-American" column now adorns the reservation.

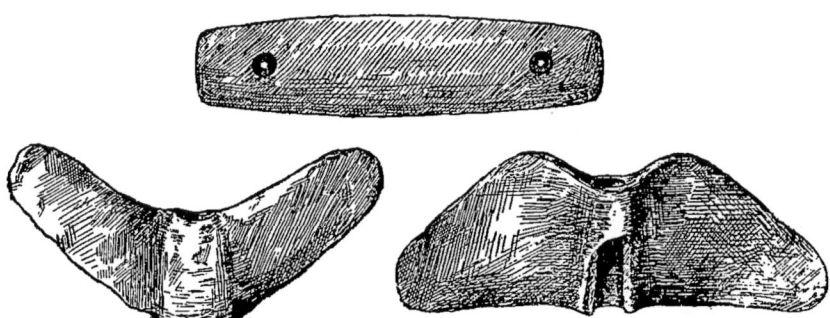

CHAPTER VI.

The Decorative and Ceremonial objects here illustrated are (above) a "gorget" of rubbed slate; and (beneath) two typical "banner stones" from Bergen County, N. J.

THE most advanced among the peoples of the earth are those whose religious observances are devoid of ostentation, and whose worship is a matter of simple faith in the Supreme Being expressed in service to mankind. Judged from this standard, the American Indian was less of a barbarian than the European of the "dark ages." His stoical attitude toward every-day dangers and the unforeseen dispensations of Providence, which are a part of life, has in it much to be commended. As well, his childish faith in the Great Spirit expresses a relation between God and man upon which it is difficult to improve. The savages of the North American continent, in common with all primitive men, were God-fearing in the highest degree. To change their "fear" to "love," and to tell them the story of Him who "went about doing good"—as an example of perfect devotion—is all that the missionaries of the white men should ever have found necessary, or expedient.

It is an accepted truth—applicable to the classic civilization of ancient Greece, to the art of the Renaissance, or to the world of today—that the handiwork of man has never been more highly developed or employed than in the adornment of places of worship or in the decoration of religious "ceremonials." Crude as was their theology, with no sanctuary save the forest glades, the wandering red men of North America gave their best, insignificant though it was, to the Chief of Chieftains. Happily, no carved sacrificial stones—like those of the Aztecs—have come down to us to spoil our conception of a people naturally kind-hearted and holding human life as having value. The Indian left no temples; neither do any traces of idolatrous worship remain. Great as was his conception of the deity, so—in contrast—are the mementos of his devotion infrequently to be found.

Natural it was, of course, that some little measure of trumpery should be associated with the religion of the Indian. Equally true it is that some among the savages, garbing themselves in skins and beaver tails and bear's teeth, should—as "medicine men"—live upon the credulity of their fellow-tribesmen. But I conjecture that these highly venerated ones earned their "board and lodging" full well, being compelled to labor with diligence and ardor; for the ceremonial orgies in which they took the leading roles were triumphs of gymnastic agility, and their "healing art" required much sound sense and a genuine skill in the compounding of decoctions. Prestige cannot be acquired, nor influence maintained, even among primitive people, without a "making good."

That the Indians at the time of the discovery of America had made considerable advances in surgery and medicine will be surprising to most readers. Yet Dean W. R. Harris, of Toronto, who has studied the habits and customs of the Canadian Indians, in his new book, "Cross Bearers of the Saguenay," writes:

> "They were acquainted with the benefits of muscular relaxation in dislocations of the limbs and knew how to replace a displaced joint. When suffering from frostbite they applied a resinous plaster. They knew how to make and apply splints to a broken arm or leg and to inject astringents into wounds.
>
> "They understood the importance of drawing blood in fevers and inflammations, employing in the operation flint knives. They began the cure of most of their acute maladies by bleeding, purging and sweating.
>
> "For ordinary colds they believed that a moderate fast was best for the patient. Anise was eaten to expel gases from the stomach. The buckeye nut and its leaves, boiled, was taken as a remedy for diarrhoea. In cases of colic they chewed the hulls of black walnuts. For fevers of a low type they gave the bark of the dogwood tree."

Fur, feathers, paint, horns, wooden masks—all these vanish after a century or two. The bones of "medicine men," chiefs, old men and children—these, too, hidden surprisingly well—are mingling with the loam of farm and village, and are but infrequently brought to light. But once in a while a "find" is made, and usually it is a stone, which throws a ray of light upon the past. I refer to the so-called "banner stones," which constitute almost the sole relics of Indian worship known to anthropologists. They are of a "spread eagle" pattern; finely polished trinkets something like a two-blade propeller, with a hole running through the middle of the specimen as though to facilitate the placing of same upon a pole or wand. Scarcer by far than tomahawk or axe, the beautiful workmanship to which they attest seems to be the pinnacle of aboriginal art. Of exceptional material, always, they belong to the class of "rubbed" artifacts. The finest specimens I have seen, outside of museum pieces, have been in the possession of farmers, found—as one is invariably told—by some grand-father "first-settler." Relics such as these, being so evidently the creations of the Indians, were instantly appropriated by the honest, though unlettered, men who tilled the soil in the days of its natural richness, and—be it told to their everlasting credit, though admittedly to my own disgust—the farmers are, for the most part unalterably indisposed to parting with them for love or money. I have seen Indian corn-bowls and pestles used by the country people as door-checks (after the manner of the carpet-covered brick of our fathers); but the banner stone is always on the parlor "mantelpiece"—an appropriate companion to the Revolutionary flint-lock on the wall over the open hearth.

Besides the "banner stone," I know of no other generally recognized ceremonial. But, as a curio of secondary interest, comes the gorget, an article of personal adornment, worn around the neck after the manner of a scapular, or tied in the hair. Broken gorgets are not excessively rare: at one site I found two fragments. Briefly described, the gorget is a crescent-shaped stone, quite thin, with two holes for the thongs which fastened it. Like the banner stone, it is invariably a rubbed specimen. Similar trinkets having but one perforation are usually spoken of as pendants. Whether gorgets and pendants once possessed a religious significance we do not know. According to Mr. Alanson Skinner, the former are still used as ornaments by the Lenapé Indians of Munceytown, Ontario, Canada.

Beads and wampum, both decorative and ceremonial, were high in popular favor among the natives of three centuries ago, but the discovery of these pretty trifles, even upon sites otherwise prolific, is of very

THE RINGWOOD RIVER
PASSAIC COUNTY, N. J.

This picturesque spot, within the confines of Ringwood Manor, illustrates a typical combination of an aboriginal and historic site. Along the banks of the shallow and rock-bedded Ringwood River the early prospectors in search of mineral wealth were guided by friendly Indians. Here, prior to 1750, Cornelius Board established iron works, which during the Revolutionary period, under the management of Robert Erskine, contributed materially to the success of the patriot cause.

The little cottage in the distance was at that time a smithy, and here, on several occasions, the horses of Washington and his entourage were re-shod.

The meadow in the middle distance would be an unpromising field for the finding of Indian remains however. Such traces should rather be sought on higher ground.

AT "MOUNT VERNON" ON THE POTOMAC

Seated within this charming little summer house upon the beautiful estate of George Washington, one beholds a panorama of surpassing loveliness. To the west, behind the observer, is the venerated mansion with its lofty portico; across the broad river are the green hills of Maryland. No finer site for a place of residence could have been selected by Augustine Washington, the father of the general, than this commanding bluff upon his "Epsewasson" plantation. Here, about 1734, he built the original manor house near Dogue Run, and here in turn his sons, Lawrence and George, developed the ancestral lands and buildings to the highest degree.

The name of the original grant is most truly aboriginal, and this lofty perch beside the great tidal river must have appealed as strongly to the primitive likings of the Indians as it does to our own supposedly aesthetic tastes; for, despite race and religion and education, man has ever possessed an intuitive admiration for the beautiful.

infrequent occurrence. Along with perforated slivers of mica, lumps of mineral pigment, fragments of pipe-stems and bowls, the diligent searcher once-in-a-while comes across a steatite bead or one or two rings of circular wampum; but anything like the discovery of a complete necklace or belt is unknown. "Trade articles"

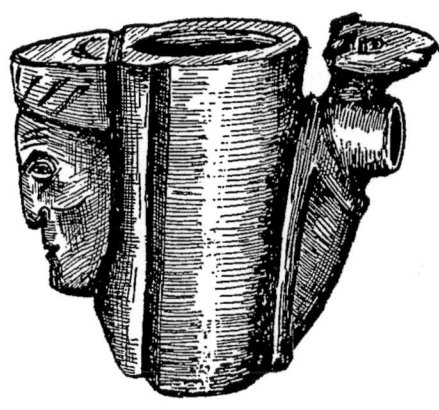

INDIAN CEREMONIAL PIPE

This interesting curio is one of the many elaborate pipes at the American Museum of Natural History, New York City.

It is of serpentine,—a most easily worked material,—and, according to museum records, was found in 1883; "having been washed from an Indian Mound, near the mouth of Salt River, Kentucky, by a great freshet at that time." Mr. N. C. Nelson, Associate Curator, says that it was evidently made, however, since the arrival of the white man, as its workmanship is not purely aboriginal.

are equally scarce. Their absence from camp site and rock-shelter may be easily accounted for. The Indians having been in contact with the settlers for but a short time—very brief indeed in point of years when compared with their long undisturbed tenancy of the coast regions—it is illogical to expect any abundance of relics reminiscent of the period of transition when Indian and settler dwelt together as next-door neighbors. Occasional *copper* arrow points have been found—fashioned, it appears, from fragments of European kettles or ladles,—and pieces of Dutch clay pipes (easily distinguishable from the more clumsy native specimens) are sometimes met with. White man's beads *have* been found, however; and no one doubts that, by means of colorful and fascinating gewgaw, the like of which the poor Indians had never dreamed, their good-will was won, and their domain shorn from them with as little delay as possible.

For years and years, however, along the constantly receding border territory, a lively traffic was carried on between trader and native. Even to this day it exists in Canada's northern wastes, with the Hudson's Bay Company a last surviver of the picturesque epoch which formed a romantic chapter in the story of the winning of a continent. The dealings between the well-established settlers and the Indians who hung longingly upon the fringes of their old homeland were, for the most part, friendly. And some of the white men, realizing that friendship and shrewd business need not be divorced, began to make wampum for the Indians which was a great improvement upon the original product. Employing crude machinery for the purpose, they contrived to turn it out in great quantity, with the result, I conjecture, that it caused a startling depreciation in tribal currency. Be that as it may, the white man's wampum is found more often than that which archaeologists would call "genuine." In the upper portion of Bergen County, N. J., a wampum factory is known to have existed about a century ago; and I know of an instance where a caché of this made-to-order wampum was found not far from Paterson, consisting of several thousand tiny cylinders of white and purple shell cores. As to my own experience, I have found no more than two or three fragments of the genuine article, in each case badly disintegrated from long burial.

Mr. Nehemiah Vreeland, of Paterson, N. J., writing for the British Numismatic Journal, has much

OLD CAMPBELL WAMPUM FACTORY

(Pascack, Bergen Co., N. J.)

This photograph, reproduced through the courtesy of the Bergen County Historical Society, shows the ancient building as it appeared shortly before its demolition in 1887. Here, for many years, the Campbell brothers carried on the manufacture of wampum, which was sold, through the medium of traders, to the Indians of the Western plains.

The curious old machine employed for the purpose is still in existence, being in the possession of Daniel H. Campbell of Park Ridge. As long ago as 1775 the industry commenced, and for a century continued to be a lucrative source of revenue. The illustrations upon the reverse of this page show some of the shell "pipes" which were drilled and polished, by the aid of the wampum machine, at the rate of four hundred a day.

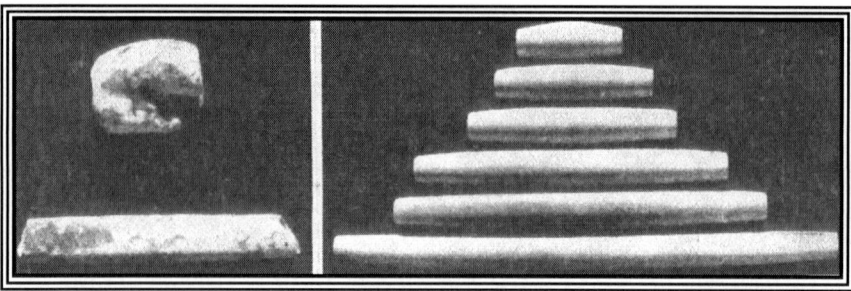

— WAMPUM —

(Photographs by courtesy of Mr. Nehemiah Vreeland, Paterson, N. J.)

The specimens at the left are genuine prehistoric wampum, found in aboriginal graves in Georgia and Florida. The six pieces of the "pipe-stem" variety are modern, and illustrate a type still in use for decorative purposes by the Indians of the Western plains. This kind of wampum was manufactured largely by the white men; it varied in length from one to six inches and was highly polished. The Pascack factory also supplied round shell discs or "moons", from one to three inches in diameter. These ornamental trinkets come, likewise, under the "wampum" classification, but have little of interest for the archaeolgoist.

of interest to say upon this subject. May I be permitted to quote a few excerpts:

> "Wampum is a bead made from the clam, periwinkle, and other shells, used in former times by the Indians of North America as money. It was also adopted by the early Dutch, French, and British colonists for the same purpose . . .
>
> The question of currency or exchange was one of the most serious problems with which the colonists had to contend, and the scarcity of the European circulating medium rendered the adoption of wampum necessary in general trade. The Dutch were the first to employ it, and it went under the names "Seawant" and "Zewant," whilst by the French it was called "Porcelaine," by the Indians "Sewan," and Wampum was the British term.
>
> It was not a cheap article of fictitious value, for the shells from which it was made were found only on the seashore, and the difficulty and expense of their supply proportionately increased their demand, according to the distance of the Indians of the interior, who used them, from the coast. Besides serving the Indian as a medium of exchange and a standard of value, Wampum was their badge of wealth and position. From prehistoric times these beads were used by the Indians for personal decoration, the number of strings worn marking the wealth and social position of the wearer.
>
> In all affairs of state the chiefs and sachems wore Wampum belts around their waists or over their shoulders. In negotiations with other tribes every important statement was corroborated by laying down one or more belts. Friendships were cemented by them, alliances confirmed, treaties negotiated, and marriages solemnized. In all of these the giving of Wampum added dignity and authority to the transaction. The red men were born traders, and it is not, therefore, surprising to find in the localities of the most inland tribes, shells that had been picked up on both the Atlantic and Pacific coasts.

The variety used by the white colonists was manufactured in Massachusetts, New York, and New Jersey. There were two colors—white and dark purple. The dark, made from the heart of the clam shell, was accounted double the value of the white. The dark Wampum was known as "Suckauhock," and in size varied from three-eighths to five-eighths of an inch long by one-eighth of an inch thick, being drilled lengthwise and strung on tendons of animals or on fibres of hemp. Suckauhock served the purpose for which gold coin is used, and the white, of half value, served in the place of silver coin.

Wampum made by the Indian in some cases was crude; for rounding, polishing, and drilling with flint or iron tools required great patience, coupled with considerable labor and skill. The drilling in some cases was performed with a bow and drill, similar to the bow-drill used by watchmakers and jewellers of the present day which certainly dates from prehistoric times.

There were several places in New Jersey where Wampum was made, Cape May and Pascack turning out the best. The factory located at the latter place was operated by the Campbell family of four brothers, who emigrated from Scotland and settled near the headwaters of the Hackensack River. In addition to being manufacturers of Wampum they were farmers.

Through the courtesy of Mrs. Frances A. Westervelt, the Curator of the museum of the Bergen County Historical Society at Hackensack, I reproduce a photograph of the old Campbell wampum factory at Pascack, N. J. (which was demolished about 1887). In Volume No. 12 of the proceedings of this body (1916-17) a thoroughly comprehensive account of this industry is given together with a valuable historic record, prepared by Mrs. Westervelt, showing how important a part wampum played in the early history of northern New Jersey.

* * *

Life, we are told, is but the antechamber, and death the door, through which all mankind passes to his greater and more complete sphere of life and understanding. Speculate as we may as to the final home of the soul, the fact remains that dust to dust returneth. And funeral rites, eccentricities of burial, and the preservation of the dead, have a strange appeal to us. Hence it is scarcely a matter of wonder that archaeologists find peculiar delight in grave-robbing under the guise of scientific research. Whether "the end justifies the means" is a matter of opinion. I myself am inclined to think that any unnecessary spoliation of burial places is sacrilegious. Better, by far, to divert our "science" into other channels than to disturb the mouldering bones of some poor creature who once upon a time bore semblance to a man, and whose skeleton housed an immortal soul.

My own experience and knowledge of Indian burials is, therefore, less than meagre. Two well-known sites have been "explored" by the American Museum of Natural History, and the results made public in the various bulletins of that organization. I refer to the finding of many skeletons at Tottenville, Staten Island, and at the upper end of Manhattan Island in the neighborhood of Seaman Avenue, Inwood. Some years ago (when I was less sentimental) I visited, in company with a friend, a traditional burial ground at Houghton Farms, N. Y., near the railway line running through the Central Valley to Newburgh. What had once been a clearing in the forest, so it appeared, we found covered with a second growth of younger trees; and here we dug, happily without result. Later on we learned that numerous archaeologists had preceded us and carried away many bones and "crania." The fact that we had enjoyed the distinction of scratching around in a bona-fide cemetery was, at the time, but a poor consolation; but this was the sum total of our recompense; not even a shin-bone did we find to reward our questionably commendable diligence. Now I am glad of it.

There is supposed to be another burial place at Sicomac, in Bergen County, N. J.; but with the supposition the matter has apparently ended, as none of the farmers in this region seem inclined to interest themselves in the matter of the bones of the long-departed. Perhaps they do wisely to hold aloof from participation in ghoulish enterprises.

Of course, it is the lure of discovery which prompts men who in other matters would be most considerate and delicate, to delve into Indian graves. As is well known, they often contain pottery, weapons, and ornaments, of considerable archaeological value-interred with the dead to serve him in the other world, or buried with him as having been inseparably connected with his life and activities. Then, occasionally, the exhumed remains reveal traces of long-forgotten tragedies. As a case in point, Dr. Abbott, of Trenton, found a skeleton in the skull of which an arrow head still remained tightly embedded, attesting to the marksmanship of some primitive bowman.

Notwithstanding all the possibilities in the way of tangible things which may be hidden in aboriginal graves, it is certain that the spirit of the red man is not to be found amid his bones. And we, being in the last analysis spiritual, and our most enduring pleasures being those of the soul, will find a more complete understanding and a greater joy in seeking the *spirit* of the Indian in the forest haunts he loved so well, and to which, perchance, he yet resorts, walking beside us, although unseen, along the sun-flecked trail.

INDEX

A.

ABBOTT, DR. CHARLES C. (*referred to*) Foreword 13, 50, 55, 104
Abundance of Indian relics............Foreword
ACKERSON, JUDGE GARRET G. (*of Bergen Co., N. J.*)................................. 30
Allegorical expressions of the Indians.... 43
Amateur Archæologists ....Foreword
AMERICAN MUSEUM OF NATURAL HISTORY (*Indian relics at*), Foreword 22, 43, 44, 78, 97
Scientific researches and bulletins..32, 103
Animals contemporary with Indian Life 59, 76, 86
Antiquity of Indian relics.......11, 12, 13, 14, 15, 16, 35
Appearance of the American Indians..42, 43
Archæology (*First principles of*)..........9, 10
The Joys of 82
(*Its scope and compensations*) 75
Argillite 8, 15, 62
Arrow-heads, 8, 9, 11, 14, 15, 16, 62, 79, 86
(*Methods of manufacture*) 9, 10, 11
(*Counterfeited by white men*) 10
(*Of brass and copper*) 76, 97
"Art" of the Indians..................................52, 53
Atrocities of the Indians........................12, 38
Awls 52, 62
Axes (*See Tomahawks*).

B.

Banner Stones 91, 93, 94
Beads and Trinkets..........................94 et. seq.
"BEAR ROCK," *Morris County, N. J.* 59
"BEAR SWAMP," *Bergen Co., N. J.*..... 63
BERGEN COUNTY, N. J. 1, 5, 9, 17, 18, 22, 49, 60, 63, 91, 98, 99, 102, 104
Indians of (*Mrs. Westervelt's account of*) 65, 102
BERGEN CO. HISTORICAL SOCIETY, (*Indian relics in possession of*) 22, 30, 102
("*Proceedings*" *referred to*) 102, 103
"Bird points" 64
"Blades" (*flint, etc.*) *manufactured by the Indians* 9
BOARD, Cornelius (*N. J. pioneer prospector*) 95
Boat-building of the Indians................22, 25
Boonton, N. J. 59
"Borers" (*See awls*).
BOSTON, MASS. (*Mural decorations at Public Library*) 28
Boys (*comments upon*)..........................16, 89
BRANT, Joseph (*Indian chieftain*)........ 26
BRONX RIVER (*Westchester Co. N. Y.*) 34
Brooks, their significance for both archæologist and the moralist........................ 19
"BUFFALO BILL" (*Col. Wm. F. Cody*) 9
Burials of the Indians........55, 93, 100, 103, 104
BURROUGHS, John (*referred to*) Foreword

C.

"Calcined" artifacts 14, 15, 16
CAMPBELL, Daniel H. (*Referred to*).... 99
Campbell Wampum factory (*Pascack, N. J.*) 99, 102

Camp Sites........2, 4, 5, 6, 9, 15, 30, 31, 44, 60, 70, 82, 90, 95, 96
Canoes, Indian.................3, 4, 22, 25, 30, 51
CAPE MAY, N. J. (*Wampum made at*) 102
Cataracts (*Their attraction for the Indians*) 26
"CEDAR POND ROCK" (*Rockland Co., N. Y.*) 71-79
Celts...41, 48, 50, 51
Ceremonial relics................................53, 91-102
Characteristics of the Indians........11, 12, 13, 25, 29, 30, 41, 42, 43, 65, 70
Chert (*Employed by the Indians for weapon making*) 8
Children (*Indian*) 13
"Chips" (*Indian waste*)........7, 8, 9, 17, 68, 78, 83, 86
CHRIST, JESUS—*His altruistic teachings and ministry*...............................40, 91
Christian Missionaries among the Indians 12, 26, 91
Civilization, its effect upon the Indians 29, 50, 76
COASTAL ALGONQUIN INDIANS, 8, 9, 13, 35, 51, 52, 53, 57, 60
Conversation among the Indians............ 43
CONWELL, Dr. Russell (*Referred to*). 63
Corn-bowls.....................................41, 45, 46, 94
CREATOR (*The Creator of Nature a lover of mankind*) 19, 20, 58
"Cross Bearers of the Saguenay"—Harris (*Quoted*) 92, 93
CUDDEBACKVILLE, N. Y....................... 68
"Culture levels"....34, 53, 67, 72, 76, 77, 78
CUYAHOGA RIVER (*Ohio*) 4

D.

DARLINGTON ROCK HOUSE........60, 63, 64, 68
Decoration of Indian pottery........54, 55, 56, 57
Ceremonials, etc. ....92 et. seq.
DELAWARE RIVER (*Indian remains beside the*) 15
(*Pre-Indian traces*) 13
DICKENS, Charles (*Quoted*) 27
Disposition of Collections of Indian curios ....Foreword
DITMARS, Prof. (*of the Bronx Zoological Gardens, N. Y. C.*) 61
DOBBS FERRY, N. Y............................... 44
DODGE, Wm. De L., artist.................26, 28
Dogs, deserving of friendship and consideration 73, 74
Dogwood (*employed by the Indians for arrow-shafts*) 11
"Dug-outs" (*log canoes*)..........................3, 51
Dutch settlers 12, 65, 97, 101

E.

EAGLE ROCK RESERVATION, (*Essex Co., N. J.*)................................... 89
ECHO LAKE, N. J. 46, 67
EGYPT (*Archaeological treasures*)........2, 3, 14, 17, 64
Elevations favored by Indians....6, 30, 92, 96
English colonists at Jamestown.............. 90
Environment of the prehistoric Americans 60
"EPSEWASSON," *Indian name of the Mount Vernon plantation*.................. 96

INDEX.

F.

ERSKINE, Robert, F. R. S. (*Ringwood iron-master and Surveyor General of the Revolutionary Armies*) 6, 45, 95

FAIRFIELD (N. J.) *Indian specimens found at* 15
Farmers, as preserving Indian curios, 7, 46, 47, 94
Farming operations (*of the Indians*).... 4
Family life of the Indians................. 44
FAYETTE COUNTY (Pa.) 38
"Feasting Grounds" of the Indians....35, 36
Fields, Indians' relics found upon.....2, 4, 7
Firearms (*Use of by the Indians*)........ 16
Fireplaces (*Apparent beneath Indian Rocks*) 79
Fishing (*Methods employed by the Indians*) 4, 21, 22, 26
Fishtraps 25
"Fish-spears" 21
Fish-hooks 21, 22
FLEMINGTON, N. J. 62
Flint (*Employed by the Indians for weapon-making*).......8, 9, 10, 11, 64, 68
Florida, Indian wampum from.............100
Folk-lore of the Indians.................29, 30
Food of the Indians.............................. 42
"Fords" (*Indian crossing-places*) 23, 25, 26
Foreign travel, delights of.................... 23
Forestry Department (U. S.)................ 30
FORT LEE, N. J. 24
FRANKLIN LAKE, N. J. 57
French and Indian War...................11, 38
Friendliness of the Indians for the Settlers 11, 12, 13, 95, 98

G.

GARRET MOUNTAIN ROCK-SHELTER (*Paterson, N. J.*)..........66, 69, 70
Generous nature of the Indians............ 43
Geological Notes........................13, 17, 18
GEORGIA, Indian Wampum from.........100
Glacial Age (*Comments upon*)......13, 17, 18
GODWIN, Capt. Abraham (*Pioneer settler of Paterson, N. J.*) 11
GODWIN, David (*His reminiscences concerning the Indians*)....11, 12, 13, 14
"GOLF HILL" ROCK HOUSE....76, 79, 80
"Gorgets"....................................91, 94
GREAT PIECE MEADOWS (*Morris Co., N. J.*) 69
"GREAT SPIRIT," Indian belief in........29, 91, 92
GREENWOOD LAKE, N. J., frontispiece 22, 50

H.

HACKENSACK, N. J.............16, 22, 30, 102
HACKENSACK RIVER.............22, 30, 102
Tribe of Indians (*Achkinkeshacky*).... 65
HAMILTON, Alexander 33
"Hand-hammers" 41, 46
"Happy Hunting Grounds" 49
HARLEM RIVER (N. Y.).................... 36
Harlem Ship Canal (N. Y.).................. 36
HARRINGTON, M. R., referred to....... 76
HARRIS, Dean W. R. (*of Toronto*) quoted 92, 93
HASENCLEVER, Peter, old German authority, quoted.................42, 43, 44
Hatchets.............................46, 47, 57
HAVERSTRAW, N. Y. 81
HENNEPIN, Father, the path-finder.... 26

Herbs used by the Indians.................... 93
"Hiawatha," the legendary genius of the Onondagas 26, 28, 29
Historical Notes: (*See "Revolutionary War"*)
Hoes, of stone, wood and shell...........44, 45
HOHOKUS (Bergen Co.) N. J. 49, 81
Horses, unknown to prehistoric Indians 51
"HORSE-STABLE ROCK" (*Ramapo Mountains, N. Y.*)...................82, 83-88
HOUGHTON FARMS, N. Y. (*Indian burial place*) 103, 104
HUDSON'S BAY COMPANY................ 98
HUDSON, Hendrick......................36, 77
HUDSON RIVER............24, 25, 36, 74, 81
Indian sites contiguous to..........24, 35, 36
Palisades 19, 24, 44
Human life held in esteem by the aborigines 92
HUNTERDON COUNTY, N. J. 52
Huts and transient habitations of the Indians.............................43, 64, 79, 80

I.-J.

Initial excursions to Indian sites............ 1
"INWOOD" (NEW YORK CITY) Indian shell deposits...................35, 36, 37
Indian burials 103
Iroquoian Pottery 68
JAMES RIVER, Virginia (*Indian specimens found at*)............................15, 90
"JAMES TOWNE" (*Experiences of early settlers at*) 90
(*Modern monuments*) 90
Jamestown Exposition, (*Arrow-making at*) 10
Jasper (*Employed by the Indians for weapon-making*) 8
JERSEY CITY, N. J. (*Indian outrages at*) 12
JOHNSON, P. Demarest (*His tale of Claudius Smith*) 84

K.

KANOUSE MOUNTAIN (*N. J.*)........... 67
KENNEBEC RIVER (*N. H.*) 4
KENTUCKY, Indian relics from........... 97
KIEFT, Governor (*of New Amsterdam*) 12
KIFT (*Egypt*) Flint implements found at 14
Knives (*flint, etc.*) of the Indians.....9, 93

L.

Lakes (*natural and artificial*) 21, 67
Lakeside haunts of the Indians............. 21
LAUREL HILLS (*PENNA.*).................. 38
"LENAPE LAND—TEN YEARS' DIGGING IN" (*C. C. Abbott*).................. 13
L'ENFANT, Major (*French Engineer*).. 33
Lenni Lenape Indians..................65, 66, 94
"Locust Lodge" (*Woodland camp*)....1, 16, 17, 18
LONGFELLOW, Henry W. (*referred to*) Foreword 29
LONG POND (*Greenwood Lake, N. J.*) 22
LYCOMING VALLEY (*PA.*)................ 38

M.

MACNEIL, H. A. (*Sculptor*) his "Sun Vow" 89
MACOPIN LAKE (*N. J.*) Indian specimens found at.........................15, 67, 68
Rock-shelter 65, 67, 68

INDEX. 109

Maize, or "Indian Corn" 42
MANHATTAN INDIANS 36
MANHATTAN ISLAND (*Indians of*)
   11, 24, 35, 36, 37, 103
   (*Shell deposits*) 35, 36, 37
   (*Indian burials*) 103
"MAN-OF-WAR ROCK" (*Orange Co.,
   N. Y.*) 80, 81
Materials employed by the Indians in
   the making of weapons: 8
   Agate 8
   Argillite 8, 15
   Chert 8
   Flint 8, 15
   Jasper 8, 15
   Obsidian 8
   Quartz 8, 15
Medicine and Surgery as understood by
   the Indians 92, 93
"Medicine-men" 92, 93
MIDVALE, N. J. 48
Migrations of the Indians 42, 43, 51,
   52, 58, 66, 81
MINISINK (*Indian settlement at*) 13, 79
MOHICANS (*Indian nation*) 26
Monogamous practices of the Indians 52
MONROE (*Orange Co.*) N. Y. 79
MONTCLAIR, N. J.—Statue of the
   "Sun Vow" at 89
MOODEY'S ROCK (*Sussex Co., N. J.*) 52
Mortars or corn-bowls 41, 42, 45, 46, 94
"Mountain-top experiences" 57, 58, 70,
   83-88
MUNCEYTOWN, ONTARIO, CANADA
   (*Indian Reservation at*) 94
Mural decoration 28
Muskrats 32
Mussels, eaten by the Indians 31, 32, 67

N.

Nature Study: 3, 5, 16, 17, 18, 19, 35, 36,
   47, 48, 57, 58, 61, 62, 64, 77, 84, 87,
   88, 105
NELSON, N. C., archæologist, quoted.... 97
Nets, as contrived by the Indians, 25, 56, 68
Net-sinkers (*Indian*) 21, 22, 52
NEW AMSTERDAM (*Dutch settlers at*)
   12, 65
NEW ENGLAND (*Indians of*) 12
NEW JERSEY'S fair-dealing with the
   Indians 11
   Indian population not numerous.......... 60
NEW YORK STATE (*Indians of*) .. 11, 26
   CITY (*Indian sites*) 24, 36, 37
NIAGARA FALLS 26, 27
NOTCH BROOK, N. J. 31

O.

OAKLAND, N. J. 81
Obsidian (*employed by Western Indians for weapon-making*) 8
Occasional habitations of the Indians
   58 et. seq.
OHIO PYLE (*PENNA.*) 38
OHIO VALLEY (*Indians of the*) 35
ONONDAGAS (*Indian nation*) 26, 29
Onondaga County Court House (*mural
   painting at*) 26, 29
ORANGE COUNTY (*N. Y.*) Indian
   specimens found at 15, 76, 79, 80, 81
ORATAM (*Indian Sachem*) 65
Ornaments worn by the Indians .. 92 et seq.
OSBORN, Prof. Henry F., referred to
   Foreword 14

P.

"Palisades" of the Hudson River 19, 24,
   44, 58
Papooses (*Indian babies*) 13, 43
PARAMUS, Bergen Co., N. J. (*Indian relics at*) 16, 17, 18
PASCACK, BERGEN Co., N. J. (*Wampum factory*) 98, 99, 100, 102
PASSAIC COUNTY (*N. J.*) 45, 95
PASSAIC RIVER (*N. J.*) 4, 9, 23, 29,
   30, 31
   FALLS 29, 30, 31
PATERSON, N. J. (*Indian relics found
   at*) 9, 11, 15, 23, 29, 30, 31, 66,
   69, 70
   (*Indian inhabitants*) 12, 13, 66, 69, 70
Patience (*a virtue worthy of cultivation*) 10, 11
Patinated specimens of Indian workmanship 14, 15, 16
"Pavonia Massacres" (1643-54) 12
Pearls (*found in fresh water mussels*)
   31, 32
Peltry, dressed and cured by the Indians 43, 51
Pendants 94
PENN, William 12
PENNSYLVANIA, Indians of 38
Pestles or grinding stones 41, 45, 94
Pictorial art of the Indians .. 28, 55, 68, 97
Pigments employed by the Indians 28,
   93, 97
PIKE COUNTY (*PA.*) 38
Pipes of the Indians 55, 64, 97
PLYMOUTH, MASS. (*Indians and colonists*) 12
POCAHONTAS 35, 90
POMPTON (*PASSAIC CO., N. J.*) 81
PONTIAC (*Indian sachem*) 26
POPES CREEK, MARYLAND (*Indian
   shell deposits at*) 35
Portraiture: rare among Indian relics
   55, 68, 97
POTOMAC RIVER (*Traces of Indians*)
   35, 96
Pottery of the Indians 53, 54, 55, 56, 57,
   67, 68, 76, 86
POWHATTAN 35
"Pre-Indian" relics 1, 17, 18
Preservation of "Indian Collections"
   Foreword
PRINCE, Prof. John D. (*referred to*)
   Foreword

Q.

Quartz, employed by the Indians for
   weapon-making 8, 15, 64

R.

RAMAPO MOUNTAINS 48, 58, 61, 80-88
   River 63, 80, 81, 83, 87
   Village 80
Religious beliefs of the Indians 30
"Reservations," allotted to the Indians
   at present 29, 94
REVOLUTIONARY WAR, incidents of
   6, 24, 34, 36, 48, 49, 80, 81, 83, 84,
   85, 95
RINGWOOD MANOR (*Passaic Co. N. J.*)
   6, 44, 45, 95
   River 6, 45, 95
   Iron Mines at 42, 95
   Early prospectors for iron 95
Rivers (*bearing Indian names*) 4

INDEX.

ROCKLAND COUNTY, N. Y. 71
Rock shelters. Frontispiece........30, 48, 59, 60, 62, 63-88
   In Europe 71
Rubbed points 62
   Ceremonials ....93, 94 et. seq.
RUSTAFJAELL, Prof. Robert de, his Egyptian researches 14

S.

SADDLE RIVER (N. J.)........1, 5, 16, 17, 18, 31
SCHLIEMANN, Dr. Heinrich, ref. to his Grecian explorations 39
SCHRABISCH, Max. references to.......9, 49, 55, 62, 68, 71, 72, 73, 74, 78, 84, 85, 86
   Quoted—facing page 1....................69, 75, 82
Scientific methods of excavation............... 76
"Scrapers" 51, 52
Sea-side habitations of the Indians......... 21
Seasons best adapted for Indian research 61, 62
Self-confidence, observations thereupon.. 19
"Serpentine," soft stone used for Indian pipes 97
Settlements of the Indians......................... 43
SHAWANGUNK MOUNTAINS, N. Y. 68
Shell Deposits..............................31, 32, 35, 36, 89, 76
Shells, used in the making of Wampum
SICOMAC, N. J. (Indian burial place)..104
"Sinew-dressers" 51
Sites favored by the Indians...................... 3
SIX NATIONS OF THE IROQUOIS..29, 81
SKINNER, Alanson, quoted......................... 94
SLOATSBURG, N. Y. 55, 80
SMITH, Claudius, "Cowboy of the Ramapo Valley"..................................84, 85
"SMITH'S CLOVE" (Ancient highway) 80
SMITH, Captain John, at Jamestown.... 90
Smoke signals 58
Smoke stains on shelter rocks..............77, 78
Snakes ("Rattlers" and copperheads).... 61
SNEDEN'S LANDING, Rockland Co., N. Y. 44
Solitary excursions not to be commended 74, 76
SOUTHFIELDS (Orange Co.), N. Y..79, 80
SOUTH SEA ISLANDS (Natives of).... 22
South-west: Indians of the...................... 53
Spear-heads 15
"Specialists" in various crafts among the Indians 11
SPRAGUE, Charles, quoted......................... 45
SPUYTEN DUYVIL CREEK.................... 36
Squaws....................42, 43, 44, 51, 52, 53, 54
STODDARD, John L., ref. to..................... 27
Stone fences 47
STONY POINT, N. Y. 71, 73
SUFFERN, N. Y. 81
SULLIVAN COUNTY, N. Y. 62
"Surface finds" 4, 17
Surgery, as practiced by the Indians, 92, 93
SUSSEX COUNTY, N. J. 52
SYRACUSE, N. Y. (Mural Painting at Court House) 26, 28

T.

TALMADGE, Rev. Dewitt (quoted)...... 18
TAPPAN, N. Y. 44
Teeth of animals used as decorations, 59, 86
"Tenth Man Brotherhood," the.............. 40
THORNDALE, DUTCHESS CO., N. Y. 49
Tomahawks..................46, 47, 48, 49, 50, 57

"Tory Rock," N. J. 48
TOTOWA (Paterson, N. J.) Indians at 12, 13
TOTTENVILLE (Staten Island, N. Y.), Indian burials at...................................103
"Trade Hatchets" 50
Traders (relations with the Indians) 36, 50, 64, 97-102
Trading among the Indians..........11, 31, 101
Trails of the aborigines........3, 5, 23, 34, 44, 74, 81
Treaties between Indians and Colonists 101
"Tree surgery" 36
TRENTON, N. J. 52
Tribes of the Coastal Algonquins........... 65
TUSCARORA INDIANS 81
TUXEDO PARK, N. Y....80, 81, 82, 84, 87

U.

Unios (fresh water mussels)................31, 32

V.

Village sites (Indian)..................4, 7, 45, 82
VIRGINIA, Indian arrows from............. 15
   Settlers at James Towne 90
VREELAND, Nehemiah (quoted upon the subject of Wampum).........101, 102

W

WALLPACK (Delaware River Valley) Indian specimens found at.................. 15
Wampum ....94 et. seq.
   Made by the white men...................98-102
   As a medium of exchange among colonists 101, 102
"War points" (so-called) 15, 104
WASHINGTON, Augustine 96
WASHINGTON, General George.........6, 95
   Revolutionary movements of....34, 49, 95
   His Mount Vernon Estate..................... 96
WASHINGTON, D. C. 28, 33
WASHINGTON, FORT (New York City) 24
Watercourses, as influencing the routes of Indian trails.........3, 4, 5, 6, 19, 20, 21, 74, 82, 95
Waterfalls, their universal appeal..........26, 30, 31, 87, 88
Water-worn specimens 14
WESTCHESTER COUNTY, N. Y. 34, 76
WESTERN UNITED STATES (Indians of the) 8, 9, 29, 51, 99, 100
WESTERVELT, Mrs. Frances A., quoted 65
   Her "Indians of Bergen Co., N. J.".... 65
   Valuable articles in "Proceedings" of Bergen County Historical Society, upon Wampum, etc. 102
WHITE PLAINS, N. Y. 34
Wigwams 21, 43
Winter, its "out-door joys"..............5, 87 88
Women (Indian).........42, 43, 44, 51, 52, 53
Woodland Exploration, comments upon 58, 61
Woodland rambles 19, 87, 88

Y.

YOUGHIOGHENY RIVER (Pa.)............ 38
Younger generation of today (Keenly interested in Indian relics)................16, 89

Z.

ZINZENDORF, Count 12

ABOUT THE AUTHOR

Historian, author, and lecturer Albert H. Heusser was born in Passaic, New Jersey in 1886. He was a member of the New York Department of Education, the National Geographic Society, the New Jersey Historical Society and Curator of the Passaic County Historical Society. In addition to *Homes and Haunts of the Indians*, he wrote a number of books on history and travel. He died in 1929 in Passaic, New Jersey.

Also available from HVA Press

Life in Sing Sing takes you behind the iron bars of one of America's most notorious prisons.

Anonymous former prisoner and author Number 1500 takes you inside Sing Sing's stone walls to see first-hand what it was really like to be incarcerated there. He tells of the day-to-day experience of prison life, with chapters on diet, discipline, famous prisoners, executions, escapes, and much more.

"With considerable literary skill...he discusses the different aspects of prison existence...."
— Publishers Weekly

$17.95 | Paperback | 978-1-948697-03-3
Available wherever books are sold | Visit us at HVAPress.com

The History of New York is the History of America™

Also available from HVA Press

"Bacon chronicles with florid descriptions ...and, above all, stories well told."

— From the foreword by Jonathan Kruk

Chronicles of Tarrytown and Sleepy Hollow tells the story of Colonial New York, its role in the American Revolution, and the myths and legends behind Washington Irving's immortal tale, *The Legend of Sleepy Hollow*.

Includes 18 black and white illustrations and a foldout map of Tarrytown in the late 19th century.

Features a foreword by Master Storyteller Jonathan Kruk, named "Best Storyteller in the Hudson Valley" by *Hudson Valley Magazine*.

$18.95 | Paperback | 978-1-948697-00-2
Available wherever books are sold | Visit us at HVAPress.com

The History of New York is the History of America™

Also available from HVA Press

A treasure trove of facts about the life and times of the American colonists.

In *Colonial Days in Old New York*, originally published over a century ago, renowned historian and bestselling author Alice Morse Earle provides a vivid portrait of the daily lives of our country's early settlers.

With a mix of anecdotes and intimate details, Earle brings America's bygone days to life.

"Her many books of Colonial life...are recognized as the best, most accurate and the fullest descriptions... of (the) life of our forefathers."
— The New York Times Book Review

$18.95 | Paperback | 978-1-948697-01-9
Available wherever books are sold | Visit us at HVAPress.com

The History of New York is the History of America™